Then *and* Now

A Series Of Biographical Essays Portraying
Changes In Culture Over Nearly A Century

Jo Ellen Oliver

Then and Now
Copyright © 2021 by Jo Ellen Oliver

Library of Congress Control Number:	2021915616
ISBN-13: Paperback:	978-1-64749-573-2
ePub:	978-1-64749-574-9

All rights reserved. No part of this publication may be reproduced, distributed, or transmitted in any form or by any means, including photocopying, recording, or other electronic or mechanical methods, without the prior written permission of the publisher or author, except in the case of brief quotations embodied in critical reviews and certain other noncommercial uses permitted by copyright law.

Although every precaution has been taken to verify the accuracy of the information contained herein, the author and publisher assume no responsibility for any errors or omissions.No liability is assumed for damages that may result from the use of information contained within.

Printed in the United States of America

GoTo Publish

GoToPublish LLC
1-888-337-1724
www.gotopublish.com
info@gotopublish.com

Contents

I. INTRODUCTION 1
II. FAMILY VALUES 5
II. RACE: Black Lives Matter 35
III. SEX: "ME TOO" in 1954 53
IV. CONCLUSION 63
Appendix A: How it all began 69
BIOGRAPHY 75

I. INTRODUCTION

I became interested in writing when I took a class of creative writing at my Houston high school. It soon became my favorite class, almost like group therapy, as students shared their secret thoughts. One day our teacher, Mrs. Baker, asked us to write about a traumatic event. I wrote about an event which had happened six years earlier, "Texas City, April 16, 1947" (See Appendix A)

    Mrs. Baker decided to enter our essays into a contest sponsored by The Atlantic Monthly. This magazine still exists, now called The Atlantic. I won second place in the United States. The young man who had won first place planned to attend another college, so the prize, a scholarship to the University of Pittsburgh, was awarded to me.

    At that time in my life, I was southern Baptist and had planned to attend Baylor University and room with my dear friends, twins Mary and Martha, who were also Southern Baptist with very high moral standards. My parents said that the decision was mine, but I knew that my dad was very worried about money. He had mortgaged the house to pay for my brother's medical school, and my sister's special education needs were also very expensive, so I decided to forget Baylor and accept the tuition-free offer at Pittsburgh.

    The University of Pittsburgh was in a beautiful skyscraper called the Cathedral of Learning. To enter the common areas was like entering an ancient cathedral, and the classrooms were decorated to reflect the many countries and ethnic groups represented in the area. To walk into my German class was like walking into Germany, perhaps the Black Forest region. When I met other students, they might ask my nationality, saying, "I'm Italian or Greek or Polish; what are you?" I usually just said, "Texan."

My roommate was second-generation French and my best friend's family came from an ethnic group in Yugoslavia.

Although the campus was beautiful, the location was very urban, consisting of bars and boarding houses, as well as a hotel and shops. There were no dormitories, as most students commuted, and the boarding houses were for students like me. I could not commute from Texas.

Although the students made fun of my southern accent, they were usually friendly. Some of my new friends might invite me to one of the nearby bars, saying, "Let's go drink our lunch." I still had strong feelings about avoiding alcohol, so I might order iced tea. The waiters and waitresses had never heard of such a thing. "You mean you want us to put ice cubes in a pot of tea?" They also had never heard of fried chicken. They could offer baked or stewed, but fried?

I enjoyed my classes and made good grades. The one exception was English. I was majoring in English and creative writing but my first essay was graded "F." The professor glared at me as if to say, "Who ever told you that you could write?" I almost packed up and went home, but my next essay was a "C" and then I began making "B's". Finally, I made an "A" and my final grade was "A" because, as the professor said, "I grade on improvement."

I had been accustomed to attending church and church activities, but here there were no Southern Baptists. There was a beautiful interfaith chapel, but because it featured all the world's religions, attendance was more like going to class than an opportunity for worship. Many of my friends were Catholic, so I went to mass with them a few times. The Presbyterians had a dinner for students on Wednesdays, so I went there a few times. In the spring a friend asked for help at his struggling Methodist church because they couldn't find anyone to teach the children. The Methodists were closer to my beliefs, so I helped teach the children until the semester was over.

I was not entirely without a moral compass. A young woman who was an assistant to the dean held freshman orientation, where we were instructed on how to behave in college, what the rules were. We also read books about the dangers of sex. Alan Paton's novel, Too Late the Pharalope, told of the danger of sex between the races in South Africa; Thomas Hardy's book, Tess of the D'Urbervilles, told of the tragedy of sex between upper and lower classes. Poor Tess was hanged for killing her baby.

Sexual mores have changed drastically in my 84 years of life, as well as attitudes about family life, race and religion. I hope to explore changes in attitudes over my life span. This is not a research paper. I taught freshman English in two universities, where the students were required to document carefully. I don't want to do that anymore. I may get a date or a name wrong. Some names I changed on purpose, to avoid embarrassing the children or grandchildren of people who behaved badly. Instead of factual research, I want to explore emotions and attitudes as they changed over the years. Why are emotions so important? We have just held a very divisive election. We are divided by politics and social mores. Yes, it is better if our emotions are grounded in actual facts; our recent election proved how dangerous feelings are when fed by lies, so I have tried to be as factual as my memory allows, but in the end, our behavior is shaped by how we feel.

II. FAMILY VALUES

Family was important to my father. He had a favorite saying, "All for one and one for all." To him, disloyalty was the biggest sin. My mother was also very interested in family, even though she had been deprived of love from both of her parents. My mother liked to brag that her ancestor, Robert Cushman, came over on the Mayflower. I researched him and found that he stayed behind and raised money for those who did come on the Mayflower. He came a little later on another ship.

My mother's ancestral and extended family were mostly gifted and talented people. Her grandfather on her mother's side was a famous painter, sculptor, and was the first photographer to open a studio in his town after photography was invented. At one time he had enough money to own part of a hotel, but evidently was not as good a businessman as an artist because he died in relative poverty. Warren Sibley Cushman (You can google him) had four children and a wife, who sadly died at age 36 from diabetes. My grandmother, Mabel Cushman, was 16 when her mother died, and it became her responsibility to be a mother to the younger children, Brian, Scott, and Charlotte, who was only six. If Mabel went on a date, always in a horse -drawn buggy, she had to take Charlotte with her.

Although the children lived in a hotel, and their father at that time had enough money, his mind was on art rather than children's daily needs. The children did not have enough to wear, and children's ready-to-wear clothing was not always available at that time. Big sister Mabel took down the hotel curtains and sewed clothing for her siblings.

Just before Mabel was 20, her father took the family to the World's Fair in Chicago, where he sold one of his paintings for $10,000, a big sum in those days. When they returned home, Mabel had a "nervous breakdown" and refused to leave her bedroom for a year. The family's explanation was that "Mabel had done too much at the World's Fair so had a nervous collapse." Years later, my mother told me that her mother had fallen in love with a young doctor, but her father would not allow her to marry him. The young man's father was an alcoholic, so Mabel's father believed that the young man was in danger of inheriting that tendency. Perhaps Mabel thought that if she stayed in her room for a year, her father might relent and let her get married. Or today we might say she had schizophrenia. More likely, it was some type of depression. When I was a child, she lived with us, and she always seemed "other worldly." She was sweet but not fully in this world.

Mabel was a talented pianist, so after she recovered from her "nervous breakdown" she became popular at concerts and parties. Phonograph music was not widely available, so the only way young people could dance was to have live music. Anyone who could sing or play an instrument was in demand. Mabel was invited to parties in the "upper crust" of society where she played the piano. She met a lawyer who played the violin, and together they made beautiful music. He was the mayor's son and came from a long line of doctors. His brother, Will, broke the tradition and went to Hollywood to write movie scripts. Thomas, himself, also broke with tradition and became a lawyer instead of a doctor. Their father was both a doctor and the mayor. His mother was descended from the infamous Rob Roy MacGregor (of Disney fame). My mother always told me that this ancestor owned many castles. He didn't own any castles, but he did live in some that he conquered and stole. Scotland placed a bounty on his head and threatened to kill any descendants, so my mother's grandmother, Clara, changed her name to Gregg and fled to the United States where she married Dr. Wright.

Mabel married Thomas Wright. She didn't love him, but she probably thought she was getting too old (over 25) and was in danger of becoming an old maid. The marriage was a disaster. Having spent her formative years living in a hotel, Mabel had never learned to keep house. She never learned to cook, and even with the help of a hired girl, her dinners were a disaster. Moreover, she didn't like sex, probably because she never loved him. When she became pregnant, she decided to abort the baby. Women had their methods, even in that day. Her husband wanted a child, so he promised to buy Mabel a huge diamond if she would go ahead and have the baby, and so my mother was born. If it were not for that huge rock on Mabel's hand, I would not be sitting here writing, and none of my siblings, children or grandchildren would exist. When her baby daughter, born on the fourth of July and called Gloria, was shown to Mabel, she said, "Take it away." Fortunately, there were loving grandparents and an aunt who stepped in to help raise the child. What did the father who wanted this child do? He left town. He went west, becoming a lawyer for the John Deere tractor company in Nebraska. They didn't divorce for 20 years because divorce would have been a scandal for someone in the mayor's family. To his credit, he did send child support, and he visited his daughter once a year. Gloria's mother Mabel always said to her, "Don't tell your father this," and "Don't tell your father that," so she rarely said anything, and the visits lasted less than an hour.

Although Mabel occasionally gave piano lessons to get a little money, she mainly depended on her estranged husband for support and sometimes did not have enough income. When her father, the artist, eventually lost his money, he moved in. I came across an old letter in which my grandfather wrote, "I am willing to support you and the child but I don't see why I should have to support your father." When my mother, Gloria, was six years old, she fainted at school and was found to be anemic and malnourished. Probably the cause was not lack of money, but her own mother's inability to cook the right foods. The extended family stepped in and invited Mabel and Gloria to dinner more often and also recommended foods like fruits which did not have to be prepared. The extended family, three grandparents, her aunt and uncle and their four children, filled in the gaps by offering love to my mother, but also spoiling her to the extent that she began to feel superior to other people. However, when alone with her mother, she felt lonely and unloved.

My father's grandfather had a plantation near the Mississippi and Louisiana border, and yes, he had slaves. The Civil War destroyed this lifestyle, as it should have, but they managed to survive in the ruins of their home. My grandfather was one of 14 children, 15 if you count the slave's son. When my grandfather, George Lafayette Gill, was in the third grade, he quit school to work in a lumber mill, where he promptly lost part of a finger. I remember having a morbid fascination with this finger when I was a small child. He married Annie Maben (I have not learned much of her background) and they moved often between small towns in Southern Mississippi, usually following lumber jobs. As they grew older, they had enough money to buy some land in Grand Bay, Alabama, where they had a garden, a horse and cow, and some pecan trees. They started to build a home on this land, but the depression took away what small savings they had, so when I went to stay with them at age four, we slept in unfinished rooms with no window glass There was a polio epidemic in Charleston, West Virginia, so our parents had sent my brother and me to the rural South. My brother George, known as Reddy for his flaming red hair, was seven.

My grandmother got water from a pump in the yard, and she cooked on a wood stove. We ate from the garden and had an occasional chicken. When I heard that the bathroom was outside, I thought it would be fun to use it. Not so much. It smelled really bad. I also thought it would be fun to help milk the cow, but she smelled terrible too. Farm life was not idyllic.

My father, like his father, quit school to go to work. However, he did make it to tenth grade. He said his school did not have an eleventh or twelfth grade. He actually started working at age nine as a delivery boy; he rode a horse to remote homes in the county to deliver from the meat market. After leaving school at age 15, he went to the docks in Mobile to work. His older brother, Spencer, had started to study engineering at Tri-State College in Angola, Indiana, but left to join the navy. He died young at age 26. Spencer did not die in battle; he died of food poisoning while his ship was docked at Galveston, Texas. My father, at age 17, had to go retrieve the body, bringing it back on the train for burial in Mississippi.

Spencer had been married, and his widow was fond of her young brother-in-law. She told him he should "make something out of himself" and go study engineering like his brother had done. Although he never finished high school, my father passed an entrance exam and was admitted to Tri-State College. His sister-in-law gave him money to get started but he had to wash dishes in the school cafeteria in order to live there. Remarkably, he finished a degree in two years and went to work for a company in Akron, Ohio, where he met a schoolteacher: my mother. She liked to tell the story of how she was eating in a restaurant with her teacher friends, and he was eating in the same restaurant with his engineer friends. The men wrote a note on a napkin inviting the women to a movie. My mother started out with one of the other men but ended up dating my father.

I will now tell a little more about my mother and her relationship with her mother." She wasn't mean," my mother said when describing her own mother to me. "She never hit me." In my mind, a lack of discipline could indicate a lack of love. Because her mother, in addition to other relatives, let her do as she pleased, my mother grew up with a sense of entitlement.

Most young people, even if they had perfect parents, will at some point disagree with how they ere raised. It's part of becoming an independent adult. With children of neglectful or abusive parents, however, the feeling is more intense. "I will NEVER do as my parents did, "they will assert. My mother had taught school for five years and really liked children, so when she married, her goal was to be the best mother ever. She resented the fact that her mother didn't provide a good diet. Consequently, my brother and I always had enough to eat. We also had nice clothes, music lessons, good children's books and toys. My father, who had a hardscrabble childhood, thought we were spoiled. He said he only ever had one toy, a little train, and he was only allowed to play with it at Christmas. Our parents sometimes fought about this issue of spending money on "frivolous" things.

My mother was not a really good cook, and she didn't like washing dishes and diapers, but she did her best. She had loved teaching school but had to quit when she married. The depression was not yet over, and school superintendents would only hire women who "had no man to support them." Even though she missed teaching, Gloria set her goal "to be the very best mother," unlike her own mother. In our early years, she seemed to have accomplished this goal, but when my brother was nine and I was nearly seven, our sister Jean was born. This was the beginning of the downward spiral for our family.

Little Jeanie was a pretty baby with blue eyes and platinum blonde curls. She seemed to develop normally although slow in walking (at 16 months). Her baby pictures seem to reveal a bright mind was there. She even spoke a few words, beginning at one year. Around 18 months she began to regress, and by two she spoke not a word and, if allowed, would spend hours rocking in her little chair or on her rocking horse. My parents thought she might be deaf, but she would startle at loud noises. She would not respond to anyone talking to her, but if someone rattled a candy dish two rooms away, she would jump up and run to get candy. She was not deaf.

If she was not deaf, she must be "emotionally disturbed." This was the name for mentally ill children at that time. My parents hired a psychologist to come observe our family to see what we were doing wrong. I did not like him; he was too intrusive. I imagined he thought I might have done something terrible to my sister to make her the way she was. This idea had already been planted in my head by my father. My sister, when angry, would break objects we cherished. For example, she might throw my mother's favorite dish against the wall or break a figurine or smash my doll's head.

"If you played with her more, she wouldn't be so bad," my father said.

"What can SHE play?" I snapped. For that, I got a slap.

The creepy psychologist found lots of things to criticize about our family, but none of it helped my sister. Nosy neighbors and friends at school were always asking," What exactly is wrong with Jean?" The assumption was that we, as a family, must have done something wrong. I am reminded of the Bible story in which the disciples asked Jesus about a blind man," Who sinned, him or his parents?" Jesus said, "Neither." Yet many people did blame parents if a child was handicapped.

A kind friend who ran a nursery school in her home said to my parents," Send her to my little school. When she sees normal children playing and having fun, she will want to be like them."

Jean was expelled the first day. She not only had screaming fits but even spit on someone. Totally unacceptable. In desperation my parents send her to a boarding school in Austin, Texas, the Brown School. It was expensive, costing my parents one third of the family income. My father, usually tight with money, was willing to sacrifice. "I will sell all I have and go live in the street if only someone will just cure her," he said.

She only stayed at the Brown School six months. She was not "cured" but did become toilet trained. She also learned to eat properly and drink from a cup. She even learned a few words which indicated how homesick she was, such as" go home," "eat dinner," and "play swing."

Because she was homesick, and also because of the financial strain, my parents brought her home. They found another school, in Houston, closer to home, which allowed (or demanded) a parent to stay with the child. A parent, usually the mother, lived in with the child. If the parent could not do this, then a nurse must be hired. At age 12, I became that nurse. My mother lived in from Monday until Friday while I went to school at home; then I stayed week ends, so my mother could go home to my father and brother and catch up on housework. In summer I stayed for longer periods. My parents did not force me to do this. I sincerely wanted to help, but once inside the institution, I regretted volunteering.

About 50 or 60 of us, parents, nurses and children, slept on cots in one huge dormitory room. Many of the child patients were in wheelchairs and had some sort of palsy, perhaps cerebral palsy or muscular dystrophy. They were called "spastic." If they could talk, their speech was garbled, and when they ate, food dribbled out of their mouths. Many, if not most, wore diapers. I panicked. "I can't do this! I can't live with all these people up close and personal!" But then I learned a valuable lesson. "Yes, you can." We can learn to live with what life throws at us.

One person who helped me get over my negative impression of this place was Tommy, a ten-year-old boy who was the sole care giver for his six-year-old brother. His job was harder than mine; he had to put his brother in and out of a wheelchair. He even had to change diapers. The father had disappeared when the handicapped child was born, and the single mother, without money or education, had appealed to the school to help her son. They allowed her to enroll without paying tuition, but only if she washed all the dishes and served as a maid. Because she was busy with all her chores, the actual care of the handicapped child fell on Tommy, the brother. He and I became best friends.

Life as a maid and dishwasher became unbearable for Tommy's young mother, so she, too, disappeared. The school let the two boys stay "out of kindness" but they let Tommy know how irresponsible his mother was. The other mothers also gossiped, and though some of them were single mothers, they were of the opinion that most single mothers were immoral.

"She probably ran after a man." some mothers said. Tommy didn't need to hear that. He knew this already.

Another friend I made was an eighteen-year-old girl in a wheelchair. Her speech was garbled, but if I listened carefully, I could understand most of what she said. Her name was Pat, and she seemed to enjoy talking to me. When I returned home, I received a perfectly typed letter from Pat. Her shaking hands would not allow her to write, but she could type, and her ideas were very intelligent. I was ashamed, because when I had spoken to her, I had talked as I would to a very young child. People with disabilities are often more intelligent than we assume. This truth also seemed to apply to my sister. She attended a reading class where the teacher used word cards and the old "Dick and Jane" primers. When it was Jean's turn to read, she would not stop until she had read the entire book. It wasn't easy; she wasn't accustomed to using her voice, so had to gulp and gasp for air, but she kept reading. I had never heard her say more than two words, so was amazed. Whether she understood what she was saying, we will never know, but obviously her visual intelligence was more functional than her auditory intelligence.

Jean did not need physical therapy and I was glad because the exercises seemed difficult and perhaps painful. Some children would cry and refuse to do what the therapist said. The therapists might then take a rolled-up newspaper and give the child a whipping. The newspaper probably didn't do any damage, but I was still shocked. One therapist, seeing the look on my face, explained. "These children have a chance to learn to walk, but if they don't try, they will be stuck in a wheelchair forever."

Years later, when I was substituting in a special education class, the lead teacher was trying to get a boy, in braces from head to toe, to stand and walk. She didn't hit him, but I thought her words were too harsh. She turned to me and said, "What you are feeling is pity-and pity never helps anyone." This "tough love" approach is less common today, but it was most evident when Jean was in school. When she was about eight, the Gilmer-Aiken Law was passed, which mandated that special education classes must be offered in public school. Before this law, a parent of a handicapped child might be told, "Now you know your child can't learn- so don't bring him/her here."

The Warburton School closed so my parents moved to Houston. Texas City, where we lived for nine years, was a small town and had only one special education teacher. This woman was handicapped herself; she had only one arm. This missing arm did not stop her from using her paddle. She explained, "They already have one handicap (mental retardation), and if we let them misbehave, they have two handicaps."

Our family moved to Houston where there were more options in special education. They still had to drive halfway across the city for her to attend the class which best suited her needs. Once Jean attended public school regularly, our family life improved. My mother was able to be a substitute teacher. She was offered a full-time teaching job but had to decline because she still had too many responsibilities with her own handicapped child. My father had the worst part of this decision to move; he had to commute back to Texas City to his job at Union Carbide.

When Jean was about 10, our cousin who was a doctor, got her an appointment at Baylor Medical School. An electroencephalogram revealed massive brain damage, mostly in the left frontal lobe. They gave her a diagnosis of Aphasia, meaning "loss of speech." Several years later my parents heard of a doctor who did brain surgery to remove damaged parts of the brain. The theory behind this surgery was: if you removed damaged brain tissue, then the "normal brain tissue" could function better. Our family drove to California to meet this doctor. He thought it would be better if this operation could take place nearer our home, so he recommended a doctor at Baylor who did the same kind of surgery. Jean was already in the hospital getting her head shaved when a staff member rushed in and shouted, "stop!" The doctors had done another scan of her brain and then decided that the damage was more scattered than they had thought and too much tissue would have to be removed. The surgery was cancelled. So was our family's hope that something could be done to help Jean.

As my brother and I became older teens, our relationship with our mother deteriorated. It is normal for teens to grow apart from parents, but our situation was more extreme. As I have said earlier, she was the best parent anyone could want when we were young, but as we became more independent, she felt threatened. She feared we would leave and no longer love her.

She even said to me," If you no longer love me, I will take this gun and shoot myself." I have, after my mother's death, perceived that she had borderline personality disorder. It may be unfair and unkind to diagnose someone after death, but doctors did not understand this condition until recently. My mother, of course, was depressed about Jean, but she also became addicted to prescription drugs and anxiety drugs. She particularly was dependent on a certain headache pill. When the doctors would not prescribe as many as she wanted, she tried to persuade me to go to a doctor and pretend to have headaches and ask for this pill. When I refused, she was very angry. Sometimes she would go to bed for days, leaving household duties (including Jean) to me.

In spite of all this, the family had good memories. Our family went to the German town of New Braunfels each year to swim in the cold rivers and enjoy the outdoors. On weekends we sometimes went to Galveston Beach for an all-day picnic. On these beach picnics, we often were accompanied by my parents' best friends, Al and Gladys Allard. They did not have children and were kind to us as children. Jean behaved better on these occasions; she loved the outdoors. My brother became an Eagle Scout, camping in New Mexico, and I went to Girl Scout camp or church camp every year. Our mother still encouraged music; my brother sang in a choir and played in the high school orchestra. I marched in the high school band. Nevertheless, her hate and love, hot and cold moods persisted. My brother complained to me," Yesterday she hated me, but today I heard her telling a neighbor how wonderful I was."

My brother, George, was clearly my mother's favorite; he inherited his musical talent from her side of the family. I was probably my dad's favorite, with no special talents but having a practical nature to work hard and get things done. My brother had difficulties with our father, who was very masculine and wanted his son to be like him. He would rather have had a son who played football than a son who played violin. Nevertheless, my father tried to be supportive and spent a week's salary (It was hard for him to part with money) on a high-quality violin.

My brother had a hernia in childhood, so could not play contact sports. The hernia was finally repaired when he was ten, but he still was not good at contact sports. He did play on the school's tennis team. His musical talent was so great that his violin teacher told my mother that he could be on concert tours by the time he was 15. George did not want to be a concert violinist, a huge disappointment to my mother.

After being disappointed that her son would not be a famous musician, our mother decided that he must be a doctor. In her family, the first boy was always a doctor, and she had been very fond of her grandfather who was a doctor. Her father and uncle broke with tradition, becoming a lawyer and a writer. This time my brother agreed with my mother; he would like to be a doctor. His grades from Baylor University were good enough for him to get into Tulane Medical School, but sadly, once there, he began to deteriorate. He failed, another huge blow to my parents, who reacted as though he had died. Our father had mortgaged the house to afford Tulane--all for nothing. It was a terrible blow to the whole family, and my mother lost touch with reality. She would tell people, "My son is a doctor."

Another sad detail of this period was my mother's delusion that my Aggie boyfriend, John, was the cause of George's failure. It seems John visited George and they went to the French quarter. George failed a test the following week, but it was only one of many tests he failed.

"If you really cared about your brother, you would break up with John," Mother insisted. I almost did what she said to keep the peace, but love prevailed. John and I have been married 63 years.

If we could diagnose my mother's mental condition, what could we say? Obviously, she had too much stress, but what was the underlying condition? Years later, when she discovered my brother was secretly married to a girl from Mexico, she went into shock, unable to speak or even move, for days. The psychiatrist insisted, "She doesn't have schizophrenia," but he did not give another diagnosis. Not much was known about borderline personality disorder at that time, the hot/cold relationships, the love/hate emotions, the fragile ego. Many years later, after my mother had died and I was working as a counselor, I read Surviving a Borderline Parent by Kimberlee Roth and Freda B. Friedman, PH.D., LCSW. I felt the author was describing my mother. Usually, these people felt unloved as children, so when they do find someone who loves them, perhaps a boyfriend, husband, or children, they hold them in a death grip,

"If you don't love me, I will take this gun and shoot myself," will always remain in my memory.

My brother was harmed more than I was by our mother's possessiveness. She might like one of his girlfriends until she feared the relationship would get serious. Then the girl was demonized. He fled to Mexico and married someone there. After he brought his wife to the United States, he kept her hidden until the baby was born. She had two children from a previous marriage, and she and George had two more. They eventually divorced but remained somewhat friendly. Sadly, he became alcoholic, and this gifted boy who was a genius in music and was supposed to become a doctor ended up doing odd jobs if he was able to work at all. His stepson took care of him until he died.

My parents mellowed as they aged. A high school friend of mine was an Episcopal priest. He invited my parents to his church, and their attendance seemed to give them a sense of peace. They had never felt they could go to church because my sister would misbehave, but she was calmer as an adult, and even seemed to enjoy church. In her final days my mother said that "having a handicapped child was a blessing because it made us better people." Sadly, I am not sure my father ever found that peace. After my mother died, he devoted himself to "saving" my brother from his alcoholism. He let my brother, who was always broke and out of work, move in with him, and he did not allow him to drink in the house. This did not deter my brother. When I went to visit, I found a stash of alcohol hidden in the garage My father's plan was not successful and my brother spent some nights in jail for drunk driving. Our father died with a broken heart. Here was a man with the best intentions who was successful as an engineer but felt unsuccessful as a family man.

With my parents both dead, I became my sister's guardian. My wonderful husband did not object to having Jean live with us. His parents had once said, "We like Jo Ellen but don't marry her because you will have to be responsible for that sister,". Having a disabled relative was definitely considered a liability in those days. Attitudes are not perfect in today's world, but much has improved. Disabled children can get free education in public schools, and in many places, parents' groups provide emotional support and other activities for the children. I found a summer day camp called "Extra Special People" in Oconee County, providing recreation and acceptance for handicapped. It was a wonderful group, and it seemed to improve Jean's self- esteem. However, the program was only available in summer, so in the other seasons I had to hire adult sitters to keep my sister so John and I could go to work and do things with our children and grandchildren.

Some of these sitters were kind to her; others were not.

I took my sister to several doctors and psychologists, and all said she was autistic, a term not known when she was a child. I had read that the brain scans of autistic people did not reveal structural damage, yet my sister supposedly had massive damage. How could this be? One doctor told me, "They get brain damage and then become autistic." Yet there seems to be a genetic component. Those with autism seem to be born into families with musical talent or families of engineers and computer specialists. Both were traits in our background. We may never know the true origin of Jean's troubles.

People with autism sometimes have a special talent; Jean's was art. She had always enjoyed drawing, painting and coloring so I began to frame some of her better paintings and bring them to art shows. The Pilot Club sponsored a yearly showing of "Artists with disability" and we participated for three years. Jean always won some prize and sold a number of her paintings. The University of Georgia had a contest, and as a result, one of her paintings was on display at the Carter Center. In Tennessee, where she now lives, two of her paintings were in the top ten for disabled artists and were hung in the governor's mansion.

My husband John never complained about having Jean in the house, but the stress of caring for her while trying to maintain a career and private family time was beginning to wear on me. A psychologist who attended our church offered to help me explore residential arrangements. His own son, also brain-injured, lived at Orange Grove Center in Chattanooga and supposedly "loved it." In addition to opportunities for recreation, a swimming pool and gymnasium, this institution offered speech therapy, art lessons and music classes. There was a new kind of speech therapy, called facilitated communication, which could either be done on the computer or done with a device similar to the game boards we played with as children. One would ask questions and the player's hands moved as though magic to letters spelling out answers. Orange Grove offered this therapy, but it has since been disproven. There are testimonies of nonverbal individuals who learned to express themselves by this method but it did not help most users. I had already explored group homes and other places in Georgia and come away depressed. Not only were most of them not appealing, but they didn't have a vacancy anyway. If I wanted to apply at a government run home, I was told the waiting time was 900 years. That many people were ahead of me in line. More resources are needed for adults with disabilities because their parents will not live forever, and even if siblings are willing to undertake the care giving, I am older than Jean and probably will not outlive her. The speech lessons did not help her, and she didn't like the art lessons because she wants to paint her own way. Nevertheless, she has a safe place to live and good medical care. Our three children have always been kind to Jean and have visited her now that I cannot drive. Our son David has agreed to be her legal guardian when I pass away.

In my work as a school counselor, most of my child patients came from homes of alcoholic, drug addicted, or mentally ill parents who may or may not have abused them. Some had parents in prison, and some did not know who their fathers were. One little boy said to me, "My parents never got married but can I come to your divorce group anyway?" Most of these children were depressed and thought no one loved them and their lives were without hope. Studies have found that if such a child had one adult mentor, a relative or perhaps a teacher, that child could survive. In my teens, when I no longer felt I could confide in my mother because of her mental problems, I talked to teachers. My church family was also helpful, and the one relative who had my interest at heart was my Aunt Dell, my father's sister.

She was the rebel of her family. Born as a middle child, she did not want to conform to her parents' strict Methodist ways. (We are Methodist now, but in those days dancing and almost any recreation was forbidden.) My aunt would pretend to go to bed early and then climb out of her bedroom window to go dancing. Her parents sent her to a girls' boarding school at age 14. She graduated and began teaching high school at age 18, married a widowed doctor at age 19 and had her only child, my cousin Don, at age 20. Don was shot down over Germany in World War Two. He was 19. My aunt inherited three stepsons who also were in World War Two, but they survived. Her doctor husband lost all his money in the depression, then died of a heart attack. Aunt Dell went to work to support the family. The youngest stepson, Charles, became a doctor when he got out of the army, and he supported Aunt Dell in her old age. When she was middle aged Aunt Dell provided a home for my grandparents. They were no longer able to do all the chores on the Alabama farm, so sold it and came to live with Aunt Dell in Tulsa, Oklahoma. Sadly, my father did not help her financially as she cared for their parents; he had enough troubles supporting our family. The middle child, it seems, is usually the one to take care of everybody else. At least, that was true for Aunt Dell and for me.

My aunt and my mother were "frenemies." Aunt Dell once told my father that he ought to leave my mother, so naturally my mother was not fond of her. My aunt would take my side if she thought my parents were being unreasonable. Nevertheless, there was some effort to get along. In my father's words, "we were Family; all for one and one for all."

I met my husband John when I was 15. A neighbor boy was attending Texas A & M., at that time an all-male college. I jokingly asked Charlie, "When are you going to bring me an Aggie?" He brought John the next weekend. My parents thought he was too old, but they liked him. (Later my mother tried to break us up.) At first John thought the same thing about me and told Charlie he was not going to date me anymore because "I was too young." He kept coming back, probably because he was at an all-male college where dates were hard to get. My parents at first would only allow double dates, either with Charlie and his girlfriend or with my brother and one of his dates. When John wanted to date me alone, my father went on a tirade, telling John he could only take me to the neighborhood theater, the Santa Rosa, and "the feature was over at 9:57 and we could have 20 minutes to get home." Unlike the young man who later tried to rape me, John actually took me to the Santa Rosa.

When I was 17, John told me he was in love with me, but "we can't do anything about it because you are too young." I would have been happy to have gone steady, but John said he didn't want me to miss graduation parties in high school, and after high school I was going away to Pittsburgh where I had a scholarship. When he visited his aunt in Austin, she introduced him to another girl who wanted to marry him, and when he visited his parents in Seattle, they got him some dates with a Colonel's daughter who was very pretty. His parents were disappointed because he didn't fall in love with her. John and I had both agreed to go out with other people, but in Pittsburgh I kept getting beautiful love letters from John. "Our" song was "Unchained Melody." Later I will describe some of my experiences with Pittsburgh boys (not all were terrible, just most), so will not repeat myself.

When I returned to Texas, I planned to enter Baylor, my original college choice, but their rules were very strict. Girls had to be in the dorm at 8:30 p.m. and they had to have parents' permission to leave campus on weekends. My parents were already trying to break us up, so I felt that if I went to Baylor, I might never see John again. I went to the University of Texas and roomed with a friend. My parents approved because UT was cheaper. The tuition was only $25.00 per semester, .and my boarding house cost $100.00 a month. I also was able to participate in my sorority, Zeta Tau Alpha, and later lived in that house. John and I continued to date each other when he could come to Austin, and I dated others when he could not. As he approached his graduation, we got engaged. I had gone to summer school every year so graduated early. We married two days after the next Christmas, December 27, 1957.

There was tension surrounding that marriage and not just because I was not his parents' first choice, and John was not my parent' first choice. My parents would have been happy if I never married anyone. I had invited some cousins, but my mother disinvited them. One set of cousins never spoke to me again. My maid of honor, a childhood friend, sewed my wedding veil and the bridesmaids' dresses, but my mother disagreed with her about how the dresses should look. One of my friends, whom I asked to pour punch, was unhappy because she wasn't asked to be a bridesmaid. Another friend, whom I asked to cut cake, was in love with the best man, but he rejected her advances. My brother, at that time in the army, was supposed to be at the wedding, but his plane was grounded, and he didn't show up. My Aunt Dell and my new mother-in-law did not like my mother's lace tablecloth, so they conspired to get rid of it and put another one on the table. At one point, my new mother-in-law and my mother shared their tranquilizer pills.

We have now been married 63 years. If a couple can survive the wedding, the marriage will probably last. Our families made the best of the situation. I have to say that John's mother was nicer to me than my mother was to him. At times my mother said she loved John and would brag on him; other times she thought he was the devil incarnate. This was her pattern in all her relationships, love and hate. John had a method of deflecting her criticism. If she said something that could be taken two ways, a nice way and an insulting way, he interpreted it the "nice" way. This was very frustrating for my mother; she was unable to insult him.

My father-in-law, John, Sr., was an army colonel. He served in World War Two and in Korea. His wife, Leatha, was very social and known for her beautiful table settings and delicious food at their parties. She was the best cook I have ever met. She was also a gifted seamstress, sewing curtains for their home and our home, and in addition, sewed beautiful clothes for me. If she didn't sew an outfit for me, she was buying me glamorous beaded sweaters and fancy shoes. I could have become defensive, thinking she was "making me over" to be more glamorous like her, but I liked all those clothes and gifts. When the children came along, she was the best grandmother, spoiling the children with attention and gifts. I think my own mother may have loved the children but was always critical of the way I parented.

When Michael was a baby, I stayed home. Mother would say, "What a pity you are wasting your education, having to do housework and wash diapers." When he was about a year old, I began to substitute teach. A neighbor lady who was keeping her baby grand daughter kept Michael. My mother's reaction was, "How could you be so cruel to leave your baby all day?" The role of women was shifting. Married women who did not work looked down on those who did, and vice versa.

When John and I married, service in the army was still mandatory; at least two years of service was required. He had applied to be in the veterinary corps, but there was a waiting period. In the interim He accepted a position of instructor in veterinary medicine at Colorado State University and I found a teaching position 38 miles away near the Wyoming-Colorado border in a small town called Nunn. There were only 75 children in the 12 grades. I taught grades 6-12, 42 in all. It was one of the most rewarding teaching jobs I have ever had. Whenever the school had a program or dance, the entire town came. It was their source of recreation, and the school was valued by parents and townspeople, even though it was inadequate in many ways. The school was too small to offer chemistry, physics, or foreign languages. Students who wanted to get into college had to find a way to go somewhere else, and they already travelled as far as 40 miles to get from their remote farms. As farm children, they sometimes had to work in the fields from 4 a.m. until 8 a.m. and then ride a bus, arriving in school at nine. They were too tired to misbehave. I never had a single discipline problem in the time I was there although a few might fall asleep. The school wanted me to start a girls' basketball team. I did not even know how to play basketball, so I bought a book of rules. Some of the girls, because of their religion, were not allowed to wear jeans or shorts, so they had to play in long dresses. We went to the state tournament in Denver and won second place in our class (small schools) in spite of my inexperience and the girls' long dresses.

John enjoyed his college teaching; I think the seeds were planted for him to later become a college professor. We socialized with other veterinarians and their wives, and on weekends we might drive into the beautiful Colorado mountains to picnic. We fell in love with Colorado and agreed that we would live there permanently someday. We no longer feel that way. As we age, we don't like cold weather, but I still think of Colorado as one of the most beautiful places on earth.

In time, John received his commission in the veterinary corps, and we moved to Fort Detrick in Frederick, Maryland. At that time, veterinarians were used to create biological warfare, mostly making vaccines for strange diseases if we were attacked. At the time it was top secret. He had to take many vaccines as well as make them. Although his work was not what he would have chosen, we had a good social life. We moved into new housing on the army base and immediately made friends with five couples on a cul-de-sac. There were probably ten couples with whom we were friendly, but the five closest neighbors became like family. A common question was "Whose house are we eating at tonight?" The couples took turns either hosting or having potluck almost every night. Only two of the couples had babies, and I soon joined them, but the social life continued. The babies could be brought to dinner and put to sleep in the back bedroom. Michael was born during this period, and I loved being a mother. The couples with whom we socialized have now all passed away except two wives, but we kept letters circulating for years. One veterinary wife, Arlene Hamm-Burr, remains on our Christmas card list. We keep in touch with her and her second husband.

After our two years with the army, we returned to Houston where John leased a veterinary practice. This had always been his goal, to have a practice, but it turned out to be less than rewarding. He was the sole practitioner so had to stay in the building long hours. Our second son, David, was born so I was quite busy. Our social life was not nonexistent but was limited by John's long working hours and my busyness with small children. John had two roommates from college living in Houston and I had a number of high school friends, whom we could see on occasion. When I only had Michael, I did some substitute teaching, but when David came along, I stopped trying to teach. For a year, I babysat my godchild, Stacy, the daughter of the maid of honor in our wedding, so her mother could teach. Stacy was two, Michael was three, and David was almost one, so they played happily.

The other mothers in the neighborhood all had children, who were usually friendly with our children. One exception was Robbie, an older child and somewhat of a bully. If my children had a new toy, Robbie would try to take it away. In today's world, children have scheduled play dates, but in our day, mothers put their children outdoors and they played with whomever showed up. John's mother had bought Michael a toy lawnmower which made a dreadful noise as he pushed it around the house. "Why don't you go show your new lawnmower to Robbie?" I suggested. Michael did that, and as I had anticipated, Robbie stole the lawnmower and took it home. It was not long before Robbie's mother brought the noisy toy back. She usually did not return things Robbie stole; her boys were so out of control she could not keep up with them. The other mothers all liked Sherry, Robbie's mother, but thought it a shame she couldn't control her kids. "It's not her fault," they said. "She is a very good mother; she spanks them every day." What they did not know, and what Sherry did not know at that time was that smoking in pregnancy harms the child. Sherry smoked during her three pregnancies and all three of her boys were born early and were hyperactive. Sherry was a nice person; she would not have smoked had she known. Later, when I was teaching, a mother came for a conference about her daughter. "I had this child when I was 14 and using drugs," she said, "but I am clean and sober now." She seemed really proud of herself.

"I am happy for you," I told her. I did not tell her that her daughter was a hyperactive nightmare, disrupting every class she was in. There were so many hyperactive children in our school that the administration did not allow us to discuss it. There was a raging public debate about whether such children should be drugged. Many mothers, including this girl's mother, refused to give their children Ritalin to calm them down, saying, "I don't want him/her to be a drug addict like me."

Living near both sets of parents was both an advantage and a disadvantage. On Michael's third birthday, both sets of grandparents showed up with a tricycle, a red one and a green one. Michael was very tactful, even at a young age. He rode both of them, not showing preference. My mother had several surgeries during this period and once stayed in the hospital six weeks. I was responsible for keeping Jean and I had some worries that she might accidentally hurt our children during one of her temper tantrums. Fortunately, she was good, but I had to be hypervigilant, constantly on alert.

John began to feel frustrated with being the only veterinarian in a practice. He had to take care of animals on holidays and weekends. One Christmas Eve, we delivered puppies in our bathtub. After almost four years in Houston, John decided to get a PhD so he could teach veterinary medicine in college. I also decided to get another degree in teaching reading. While we had lived in Maryland, I had endured a frustrating year trying to teach high school English because about a fourth of my students could not read a simple sentence. I did not know how to help them, so of course they did not behave well. Many dropped out to work in a mill. There was no special education in that system, and all children were supposed to use the same curriculum. If I were ever going to teach full time again, I would need to know more.

Both sets of our parents thought we had lost our minds. Didn't John have a doctorate already? Why did he need more education? And as for me-I was a mother and should be concentrating on my own children instead of other peoples' kids. In spite of all the protests, we headed to Auburn, Alabama. In spite of being dirt poor, we were happy there. We were not entirely without income. John had a stipend from the Scott Ritchey Foundation, and I taught two classes at Auburn University and sold Avon on the side.

This period of time (1962) was the beginning of women's liberation. In my first teaching job (1958) the superintendent had told me, "I am going to pay you $100 less per month because you have a husband to support you. Men need more because they have to support their families." It did not occur to him that women had families too. My yearly salary was between $3,000 and $4,000 per year. I have mentioned elsewhere how we coped with having a low income. As for women's liberation, I was not a fanatic but did want to work, at least part time.

My best friend, Collie, thought I should stay home; "You only have your kids about 20 years; then you can do what you want." I noticed, however, that many married women who disapproved of working mothers still hired babysitters so they could go shopping or go play bridge. They claimed to need outside stimulation, so what was the difference in what they were doing and what I was doing? Even to this day, I sincerely believe that women who have small children are happiest if working part time. Some work provides intellectual stimulation and opportunities to socialize, but full-time work puts a terrible strain on the ability to be a good parent. Nevertheless, many women have to work full time; they do not have a choice. A bigger issue is that today' women want to be the CEO, and that cannot be accomplished by working part time. There is no reason that women cannot be president of a corporation or become a high-ranking government official if their children are older. I applaud their ambition. Some women postpone motherhood until they are almost 40 and have achieved their career goals. The good news is that older parents are more mature and in a better financial situation. The bad news is that there is a slightly higher risk of having a child with a disability, such as autism or Downs syndrome.

I have already detailed in other sections of this book how race relations were boiling over at this time and how we fit into that pattern. One reason I was so happy in Auburn was I seemed to have it all; I went to Auburn in the mornings to teach and learn, leaving the children with Amelia, our maid and babysitter, then came home at noon and spent the afternoons playing with the children and doing things they wanted to do. Another reason for our happiness in Auburn was the Eubanks family. This mother and father of four, who lived one block away, were friends of our family. Our children were similar in age and played with their children almost every day. At least once a week we cooked out in their yard or ours.

We had less interaction with extended family because we were in Alabama, and they were still in Texas. However, my mother decided to pay a visit on the week that we were particularly in a financial bind: no groceries and no money to buy some. I knew that if my mother was aware of the situation, she would be sure to amplify her theme about how foolish and selfish we were to go to graduate school when we had family responsibilities. My friend, Collie Eubank, gave me a roast from her freezer and another friend, Jean Kummero, gave me a cake she had made. Amelia brought vegetables from her garden, and I made a big pot of vegetable soup. I told Mother, "I know how you love soup, so we are having it every day."

In addition to the Eubanks children, Michael and David played with Mark McCullers, who lived across the street. The mother, Gail, was a counselor at Auburn University, and my friendship with her and another friend, Gloria Terrell, who was a counselor in public schools, inspired my interest in counseling. I took some courses in counseling along with reading and English.

I have written about the traumatic birth of our daughter Julie in another section of this book. Because I was very weak from loss of blood, the hospital told me that I must hire a private duty nurse, but we had no money. Our friend, Jean Kummero, was a nurse and she came for free. I will always remember our wonderful friends from Auburn.

I finished my masters' thesis in my hospital bed and graduated My mother had wanted to come and take care of me after the birth, but I did not want her. I felt too weak to fend off her psychological attacks, so I told her I was doing very well. She said that if I was really doing well, I could keep my sister Jean while they went on vacation to Mexico. I felt I had to agree, or my lie about how well I was doing would be exposed. Jean arrived on the next plane. For the first time, John was angry about having Jean in the house. "If your parents really cared about you, they would not have sent her." I don't know that they didn't care; they just were obtuse and self-centered. And they needed a break from Jean.

I had to be hyper-vigilant to protect my three young children, including a tiny, nursing baby, from Jean's unpredictable moods. At her home, she had a bicycle, so I assumed it was safe for her to ride a bicycle in our dead-end street. What I did not know was that Jean's bicycle in Houston had hand brakes and the bicycle I borrowed for her had the old-fashioned brakes. She crashed and fell, breaking her hand and sustaining other bruises. It was a tiny, hairline fracture, and even though my doctor took an X-ray, the fracture did not show up. Later, my parents' doctor took an X-ray from a side view and saw the tiny fracture. My parents accused me of neglect and much worse. Some kind neighbors had told me that Jean could play on their children's play scape; she was obsessed with swings. The problem was the playscape was too small and not properly anchored, so there was a danger that Jean, because of her adult size, might turn the whole thing over on top of small children. I told her she could not play there, and she became angry. To distract her, I told her she needed to iron some clothes for me (She actually enjoyed ironing.) Unfortunately, I forgot she was left- handed, so when she tried to iron with her left hand, it hurt and threw her into the worst tantrum I had ever seen. She kicked our poor dog until he ran away for two days and smashed the gate in our yard., so I stayed in the basement with her while John kept the children upstairs. I lost my milk and could no longer nurse. My parents were due home, so we arranged for Jean to fly home. I tried to warn them on the phone about her sore hand and bruises and they didn't seem too upset, but I also felt compelled to write a long letter detailing her temper tantrum and suggested that they should find a residential treatment center for her. This angered them so badly that they accused me of terrible things. They said I had ruined her hand and that she would never paint again. "She had only one talent, and you took it from her." They also threatened to sue my doctor for not finding the fracture. I did not speak to them for six months. We eventually reconciled on Christmas day, but I warned my mother that if she ever brought up that subject again, we would have no relationship.

The whole episode with my parents triggered a post-partum depression. I had to take down the pictures my sister had painted, because when I saw them, I burst into tears, and when I didn't see them, I still burst into tears. Because I now had a masters' degree, I was offered a full-time teaching position, but I was in no condition to accept. Why didn't I go to a doctor and ask for help? In those days, mental illness was a terrible stigma. People were put into hospitals without their consent. I was afraid that a doctor might declare me mentally ill and unfit to be a mother and I would lose my children. My children and my husband saved me. They did not deserve a depressed mother or wife, so by sheer will power I banished the despair that was in my heart. I will never belittle anyone with depression. It's a terrible, oppressive feeling.

Michael enrolled in a wonderful kindergarten, and I got involved making costumes. The teacher was Mrs. Meagher, and she operated the kindergarten in her home. She did not have a college degree, not a requirement in those days, but had taken a few classes at Auburn. What she lacked in education, she made up for with creativity. The children loved her school. Some of her pageants would be called "politically incorrect" today. One of the costumes I made was an Indian costume.

I still continued to sell Avon, taking all three children with me. Michael and David carried my samples, and I carried the baby. People bought a lot of Avon, maybe because they felt sorry for me.

One other scary event happened in Auburn. When Julie was ten months old, she developed a high fever, 104 degrees. Our doctor had seen one case of spinal meningitis the day before, and he was afraid that Julie might have this disease. He told us to take her to the hospital and he would meet us there. When the hospital heard that our doctor thought it might be spinal meningitis, they told us that because it was highly contagious, they must prepare a special room where she could be isolated. They then told us to go wait in the hospital waiting room, where other people were gathered. I tried to get in the farthest corner away from other people, but as the minutes continued to pass and the baby seemed to get hotter and hotter, I stood up and yelled, "My baby is dying, and no one is doing anything." An evangelical preacher who was in the room jumped up and commanded everyone to "pray for this baby." Some began mouthing prayers. I guess it helped because it got the attention of hospital staff. They rushed out and dumped the baby into a tub of ice water to lower her fever. Soon we were in isolation. She was in the hospital ten days, and nobody could diagnose her disease. Spinal meningitis was ruled out, but the high fevers came back each day. On the tenth day, she broke out with chicken pox, but only with a few pustules. The staff explained that when someone has chicken pox without breaking out, it goes inward and causes more harm. The fevers stopped and she came home.

John had decided he loved research, especially in the area of neurology, so off we went to St. Paul, Minnesota, with three children, six, four, and one. The children were excited that they would have an opportunity to play in snow, but as soon as they went out in it, they returned immediately. "That stuff is too cold," they complained. Nevertheless, the boys learned to ice skate and play hockey. The fire department would come out as soon as freezing weather began and flood areas behind schools and behind our housing complex.

Finding housing was a problem when we first moved to Minnesota. We had applied for student housing on the university campus but did not get accepted. Therefore, we had to look for an apartment. Most apartments insisted on "no children" and those who did accept children said, "no more than two." We considered hiding one child in the car while we applied for apartments, but of course that was not an option. We finally found a town house that allowed three children. It was beyond our budget, but we managed somehow.

As a mother, I had to adjust to dressing children for the outdoors. In addition to waterproof snowsuits, children needed two pairs of mittens, two pairs of socks and a hat which covered all the face except eyes. Snow boots had to be bought large to accommodate the feet growing, but if too large, they would fall off. I sometimes greased their faces with Vaseline to protect the skin under those hats covering faces. Sometimes, after getting dressed for outdoors, a child might say, "I have to go to the bathroom." And, when they came in, they dripped melted snow on the floor. We had to have racks of things drying all the time, and the smell of wet wool was in the air. Minneapolis had the first indoor mall I had ever seen, so I sometimes took the children there to run through it.

There was a skating rink right behind Michael's school, and since it was only a block from our home, I sometimes let him go with older children. One snowy day, a neighbor boy of ten, Ole, knocked on the door. "Can Michael come skating with us," he asked. A group of other neighbor boys was with Ole. Although Michael was only seven, I said, "yes," but said, "if you look after him." They were gone less than an hour when a blizzard began. I saw Ole pass by our window, so stopped him. "Where's Michael?"

"I don't know. Back there, I guess," he said pointing toward the school, which could no longer be seen.

Alarmed, I grabbed my coat and other gear. David, age four and a half, was watching cartoons. Julie, at 18 months, was at a dangerous age, able to fall downstairs or swallow something harmful. I packed her warmly on my back and told David, "Do not move from that TV until I get back. I have to find Michael." I staggered towards the school and found Michael crawling on the ground. After skating, people took off skates and put their boots back on. Michael's fingers had been too numb to unfasten the skates, and since he could not walk in the skates, he was on the ground. I had also packed a thermos of hot chocolate for him, but his fingers were unable to open it. I dragged him into the hall of a nearby apartment building, across the street from ours, and began to undo his skates. Those of us who have lived in frigid climates know that if a hand or foot has started to become frozen and then thawed out, there will be sharp pains as that part of the body warms. Michael began to howl as he warmed up. Several adults poked their heads out of their apartment doors, and asked, "Who are you and why are you abusing that child?"

"I am trying to thaw him out," I explained. Several of these people were native to Minnesota and knew about these things, so they examined his feet and reassured me.

"His feet are blue," they said, "and that means he will be all right. If they had turned pure white, he might have to get them amputated." (I may have the blue and white reversed, but I think that is right.) After Michael was significantly warmed, I got him back to our apartment across the street, Julie still on my back. David had been good. He had not moved from the television.

Although our house was a town house, it was connected to the other houses through the basement. Our laundry was also in the basement. I thought it was all right to let the children ride tricycles and play in the basement, not realizing it was not soundproof. Their voices reverberated through the other apartments, and soon we got complaints about our noisy children. We gave Michael a birthday party and invited seven little boys. Of course, they made noise. Our childless next-door neighbor came over to complain. "Your children are making the pictures fall of the wall," he growled.

"If you think it's bad over there, you should be over here," John replied. The neighbor did not appreciate our humor. These neighbors soon moved. I was happy when a couple with two children moved in. I decided to become friends with this wife, but soon we heard strange noises from next door. The wife confided in me that her husband beat her.

"I'm going to ask a favor of you," she said. "If you hear noises of banging and thumping and me screaming, will you please call the police?" It was a strange request.

"I know I have been a nosy neighbor before," I told John, as I stood with my ear to the wall, "but nobody ever asked me to call the police." Fortunately, we did not have to call for help. She kicked that husband to the curb.

I made friends with another neighbor who had a son the age of David. Since Michael went to school, it was nice to have a friend for David. His name was Mike, so we called him "little Mike" to distinguish him from our Michael. His mother, Nancy, was a widow who had married an older, divorced man. The man's ex-wife was not happy that he had divorced her and married a younger woman, so one day we saw him running past the apartments with the ex-wife chasing him and beating him over the head with her purse. Spousal abuse is not limited to men as the aggressors.

After a year, we became eligible to get into student housing, which was cheaper and more convenient. Student housing was an international community, an education, not only for our children, but for us. Our new best friends were from Australia and our boys' best friend was from Pakistan. I say that the boy from Pakistan was a best friend, but he and my boys were more like "frenemies." The little boys played rough, and the Pakistan boy dropped David on his head, causing a concussion. Later, David pushed another little boy (from St. Paul) down, causing a concussion. Still later, while playing football, our boys caused the Pakistan boy to break his arm. None of these accidents was intentional, but all required visits to the doctor and an angry parent from Pakistan. We all apologized and made international peace. When David received his concussion, the doctor said, "Do not run and play for several days." David asked permission to go outside and watch the other kids play. I said, "Yes, but stay seated the whole time. Do not get up and play." A few minutes later, I went to check on David. He was nowhere in sight. Finally, I spotted him, sitting on the roof of the apartment building.

"You were only supposed to sit", I admonished him. "I am sitting," he replied, and I can see better up here." Raising boys is an adventure.

I was offered a job to teach freshman English at the University of Minnesota, and because the boys were both in school and our friends from Australia offered to babysit Julie, (they had twins the same age), I was able to take the job. I have described this period in another section of this book.

Our political views changed some during this period. Both John and I were raised in staunchly Republican families and our Southern friends were all conservative. Minnesota was extremely liberal (at least in those days). Think Hubert Humphry, and you get the idea. We had to admit that public life seemed better where taxes were higher and public services were better. The level of education seemed higher, and even those public servants who worked in low-paying jobs might be reading Tolstoy as they rode the bus. Our kids took free classes in the summer. Public parks were kept immaculate, and on and on. I know Minnesota is a different place now, especially in the aftermath of George Floyd's death, but in those days it seemed ideal. The Methodist Church we attended was all about social justice, and the ladies' group I attended didn't just drink tea and discuss religion; we went to the jail and insisted they improve sanitary conditions. We never became as liberal as our Minnesota friends, but we are no longer in agreement with our conservative friends. There is something appealing about the conservative ideals of self-reliance and not depending on welfare, of taking care of one's own family, of working hard, of staunch patriotism, but as a Christian I cannot turn my back on those who are poor, disabled and marginalized. I think we should banish the words "liberal" and "conservative" and all work together for the good of everyone.

After working at the University of Minnesota, I worked for a few months in the institution for mentally ill children. John worked long hours on his research, and after getting his doctorate, we set off to Athens, Georgia. In Athens we owned our first, really nice house. It had five bedrooms and the children could each have their own. They had been accustomed to sleeping together in one bedroom at our tiny apartment in Minnesota. Now they could each have a room, but they still chose to stay together. They would ask each other, "Whose room shall we sleep in tonight?" Then the three of them would head off into one of the bedrooms.

After seeing how advanced the schools were in Minnesota, I was disappointed by the schools in Athens. The children's bathrooms at school were so dirty that some of us mothers took turns going to the school and cleaning them. It really isn't fair to judge the Athens schools at this time because they were in turmoil due to integration. I have already written in another section of this book about Julie's unhappiness in first grade. David, however, thrived. His teachers, both black and white, appreciated his intelligence and used him to help teach. When the state opened a program for gifted children, David was one of the first children selected. Michael said, "If they had it for my grade, I am sure they would have picked me." I think he was right. They started the gifted program at lower grades. The gifted program was held in summer, and David did not want to go to summer school. We made him go; I think he enjoyed the challenging curriculum. The school also started a music program and David played a cello, almost as big as he was. In addition to school the boys participated in Little League sports and Julie was a cheer leader.

When John and I married, John said he wanted two children and I said I wanted four. We ended up with three, but that was about to change. John had a godchild who at age 15, had ended up in jail for possession of drugs. Her mother did not want her back. Her father, who had divorced and remarried, did want her back but the stepmother, who was only a few years older than her stepchildren, did not. Cathy had a phobia about going to school. Her uncle, trying to be helpful, had marched her to school with a belt. He did not realize she hid in the janitor's closet instead of going to class. Cathy's mother asked us to take her for the summer. We did, and she was delightful, causing no trouble, but when she returned home, she was in trouble again, ending up in a foster family. We took her again and began a wild adventure. We were supposed to keep her only for the next summer, but her mother refused to take her back. Her father still wanted her, but she refused to go to him. Her heart was broken that her mother rejected her, so we kept her for two more years.

She identified with the hippie movement and would wear long, flowing robes and go barefoot. We tried to be tolerant about clothes. "What is on our outside is not as important as what is on the inside," I tried to believe. Didn't Jesus say, "Take no thought of what you will wear"? The school was not so tolerant. They put her out for violating dress codes. She did not refuse to go to school, but the only class she liked was art, and she often skipped the other classes. We would have to leave work to go to the school in order to get her back in. As a hippie, she shared their values, both good and bad. We agreed with their values of "love and peace" and the value of loving people over money, but we did not think it was all right to take drugs and to stand on the corner and beg instead of going to work. We also didn't believe in "free love" and unmarried sex, so had to chase several of her boyfriends away. "This is not the whorehouse," I told one hippie boy. She was very intelligent; that was not her problem. She was talented in art and could write beautiful poetry. She claimed to love children and got along with our children, but this was also a problem in our minds because we didn't want our children to adopt her values. Michael was the most sympathetic to her lifestyle. He was just a few years younger than Cathy and shared her love of rock music. He resented that I turned her away. Her emotions were the cause of trouble, so we got psychological help. We also had to take a stand and tell her that we would not support her after she reached the legal adult age of 18 unless she was in college or preparing for work; then we would offer some help. She graduated from high school and chose not to get more education, nor did she have a job. I told her she had to leave. I feel some guilt, even to this day. I once wrote her to apologize but my letter was returned unopened. Her own mother had rejected her, and so had I, reopening the old wound.

John felt we should have kept her until she was 21, but I was living in the shadow of my sister's disability: I knew someday I would be responsible for an adult, my sister, who could not support herself and would also need personal and psychological care. I did not want two such people in our lives. As if we didn't have enough with our children and Cathy, we briefly took in another child., a nine-year old boy who was friends with our boys. This little fellow would come home with our boys after school and was in no hurry to leave. When I suggested he call a parent to ask if he could stay so long, he never got an answer on the tele phone. He was living with his biological father, who worked two shifts at the poultry plant and evidently drank quite a bit on the weekend.

One day, Bobby asked if he could live in our tree house. We told him, "You don't have to sleep out there; you can come inside." It seems that the mother was in jail for stabbing the stepfather, and Bobby was sent to his older biological father, who was unable to provide supervision. He never wanted to go home to his father's trailer. Bobby begged me not to call the Department of Family and Children's Services, saying "They will put me in a foster home with mean people." He had experienced this situation before. I called the agency any way, and they agreed that we could keep Bobby.

John, who claimed to only want two children, was the one who said we should take Cathy and Bobby into our home. So now we had five children. Bobby was always polite and well-behaved, but he did not stay long. His mother was released from jail and was able to get him back. After Cathy left, she lived with a boyfriend and eventually had a child.

Another child who spent a summer with us was my brother's stepson, Juan. He had difficulty in kindergarten because he could not speak English. He did improve and learned to read.

I have written in other sections of this book about my unhappy teaching job and my wonderful experience with Follow Through, the federal program for disadvantaged children. John was becoming a little dissatisfied with his position at UGA, so when asked to become department head at Purdue University in Lafayette, Indiana, he accepted.

I did not want to go to Indiana, and this was the beginning of tension in our family. John was thrilled with the honor of being department head, and the children liked their Indiana schools better than the ones in Georgia, but I was miserable. We had left a beautiful new home in Georgia and now moved into an old rental home, owned by Purdue. It had bats in the attic and rats in the cellar. We eventually moved into another Purdue-owned home in the middle of the university's horticulture park, which was better. It was without bats and rats, but still hard to clean. The home had been built in 1906 and had a front and back staircase, as well as many ornamental features. I should have been thrilled to live there, but the home was hard to keep clean. I missed our cleaning lady in Georgia. Indiana wives evidently didn't believe in being lazy; they thought a wife should clean her own house.

We also had lived in a subdivision with wonderful neighbors, such as Dave and Gale Anderson, in Georgia. Our children had been accustomed to walking to school and having playmates nearby. Now, even though we were surrounded by a beautiful park, if the children wanted to play with a school friend, I had to drive ten miles down one road or five miles down another. Even the school was ten miles away, so sports practices became a commuters' nightmare. Life seemed harder in Indiana, but the children loved living in a park and would try to visit the outdoor weddings which were sometimes held in the open. Their father and I had to tell them, they and our dog, Rascal, could not have a share of refreshments with the wedding guests.

The other veterinary wives in the department were not friendly at first. They thought my husband's position should have been awarded to their husbands. They eventually warmed up; it seems midwestern people take more time to decide if they like a person, so we ended up with some friends. I eventually got a job teaching first grade, and some of those teachers also became friends.

A scary incident which happened was my hysterectomy. In the middle of the night at the hospital, I lost a large amount of blood. The nurse told me I would die if the doctor did not come, but she could not persuade him to come. She pushed me closer to a table with a telephone. "Call your husband," she said, " and tell him to come up here and demand something be done. If I call, I will get fired." The hospital was locked up at night, but this nurse told me she would sneak down to the emergency room and unlock one door. "Tell him to come to the emergency room."

I called John and he came. Before he arrived, a new nurse came in and said, "My God, she's in shock." My blood pressure was 30, at least one of the numbers anyway. The new nurse also called the doctor, and by that time he had decided he needed to come. He and John arrived at the same time, and I was taken to surgery.

I want to take a minute to describe how it felt to be on the edge of dying. Some people who have written about near-death experiences have reported seeing something, either God or angels or dead relatives. I did not see or hear anything, but I felt euphoric; it was blissful. I must have said something about Jesus, because a staff member said, "Do you want the priest?" I declined. This was a Catholic hospital, and the priest had been to visit in my room several times. He was a really nice fellow, but I got the idea he felt that if I were not Catholic, I would go to hell. He would feel bad to watch me die, especially if I refused Catholic rites; I didn't want to hurt his feelings.

I am glad I had this near-death experience because I think I will be less afraid when the time comes. We will all die. I do not look forward to the causes of death, what comes before: sickness, pain, accidents, fires, but the actual passing can be euphoric.

It took almost a year to recover from the hysterectomy, and here again, there were psychological effects. Although we didn't need or particularly want any more children, I was saddened that I could no longer have any. I avoided baby showers or pictures of cute babies.

The next year John was offered the department head's position back in Athens, Georgia, so we returned and have been here ever since. Georgia is now our home.

II. RACE: Black Lives Matter

In January 2020 Our thirteen-year-old granddaughter, Rachel, asked for my help. Her class at school was studying civil rights and race relations. When they heard that her mother Julie was born in Alabama, they were horrified. Even worse, they learned that her grandmother (me) grew up in Texas, lived in Alabama, and now was living in Georgia. Although Oregon has its own history of racism, they wanted to know more about how it was to live in these "racist" states.

    Dear Rachel,
    I understand that you are studying civil rights. In the next day or two, I will write you stories of growing up in the South and how people and attitudes changed. I was born in 1936, and at that time not only schools were segregated but businesses and public buildings had separate waiting rooms, rest rooms, and water fountains for blacks and whites. Some businesses did not even let black people inside. When I was about 10, I was eating in a restaurant with my parents when a black family came in. The manager met them at the door and turned them away. I remember feeling sorry for them but did not know what I could do.
    I was born in Ohio, which at that time did not have many people of color. We moved from Ohio to West Virginia and then to Galveston, Texas, when I was four. A year later we moved to Texas City, a town between Houston and Galveston. Our small town had a separate elementary for black children. We had a large Mexican population. They attended "white" school but

always sat at the back of the classroom and spoke Spanish. Our family knew a teenage African American boy who wanted to attend high school but there was none in Texas City. He had to get up at 5a.m.and take a Greyhound bus to Galveston, where there was a high school for blacks.

Today, the use of the "n" word is totally unacceptable but when I was a child, everybody said it, even black people. I must have been eight or nine when someone explained to me," It's more polite to say 'colored people.'" Once my aunt said something about "a black woman" and my mother said, "It's wicked to call somebody black." Later the term "colored people" became offensive to people of color and in the 1970's the "black is beautiful" movement began. Once when my father came to visit and used the "n" word, I said, "Daddy, please don't say that-I don't want the children to learn it." He looked perplexed and then said, "So what should I say?" Your mother (my daughter) would say, "Don't say anything. A person's race is not relevant." Yet we know that race matters. My teaching partner (who is black) told me she prefers "African American."

My father would be condemned as a racist today. He not only used the "N" word, but he was against integration. Yet I remember his going to the hospital to pay the bills for some black man he knew. One night when I was about 10 years old, my mother, my aunt, my father and I were driving through a "black" section of Houston after attending a concert. Suddenly a black man and woman ran into the street. The man was trying to stab the woman. My father jumped out of the car, and I followed him. He tackled the black man who dropped his knife on the pavement. The man reached for the knife and my father stomped on is hand., then jerked him to his feet. The woman's hands were dripping blood and she grabbed my father's white jacket, imploring, "Save me; save me." The man had been trying to slit her throat, and she had used her hands to protect the throat. Now her hands were sliced open.

My father told me to go into a bar and tell them to call the police. It was Saturday night in an all-black bar. The last person they wanted to see was a little white girl. It was hard to get the bartender's attention. He finally said, "You don't belong in here little girl. Where are your parents?" When I told him, my father was outside with a killer, he reluctantly called police. There was no love lost between the police and the black community, even then, but the police came, and the woman was able to get to the hospital nearby, where she actually worked as a nurse. Her ex-lover had been waiting as she came off her shift.

I have lots of stories to tell you how things changed (Although sadly, some attitudes haven't). More later. Love, "Magra"

Dear Rachel,

I promised to write more about civil rights, so here goes: The Brown versus Board of Education happened in 1954, the year I was a senior in high school. This court decision made it illegal to have separate schools for black children. Although I had always been sympathetic to the plight of black people, I did not think integrating school would work; I could imagine fighting and people getting hurt if half of our school consisted of black students. I could not imagine the white population (given the attitudes of the time) voting for a black girl as football sweetheart or "most popular." I realize now that these so-called honors are shallow and superficial, but to a teenager they are important. I thought African Americans would be better off in their own school. Fast forward thirty years. All of our children went to integrated schools, and yes, a black girl did get elected to football queen and most beautiful, and half of the cheerleaders on my daughter's team were black. Change can happen.

My first experience at an integrated school was at the University of Pittsburgh where I had a scholarship. For the first time, I studied with black students, but things were still not equal, for women as well as blacks. I had loved marching in a band in high school, but Pittsburgh had an all-male band. They also did not allow majorettes. Some of us girls who had been leading our bands in high school decided to petition the school to let us march. We formed a majorette club and met once a week to practice our routines. One of our twirlers was black. One day I was shocked to overhear two girls talking, "If the University lets us march, we must find a way to get rid of ___ (the black girl)". I had been naïve to think attitudes were different in the North. The University of Pittsburgh would not consider our request. None of us marched. I even offered to play my horn instead of twirling my baton, but they did not want girls.

Back in the South, most schools decided to ignore the mandate to integrate until President Eisenhower sent troops to Arkansas. More later.

Love, "Magra"

Dear Rachel,

A few years after your grandfather and I married, we moved to Auburn, Alabama, to pursue masters' degrees. He already had a Doctor of Veterinary Medicine degree, but to teach in a university one had to have a master's and preferably a doctorate in a specific area of veterinary school. I had been teaching high school English but was unhappy with the students who did not read well enough to do their assignments. I wanted more expertise to help these students. I got a job teaching remedial reading to college students who were failing English and took classes to learn more methods. My hours were fairly short-from 7 a.m. until noon although your grandfather's hours were longer: 8 a.m. to 6 p.m. We hired an African American lady to baby sit Michael, 4, and David, 1, during those morning hours. One day David became sick, and Amelia could not reach us. This was before the days of cell phones. Amelia took David to the doctor but had to sit in the colored waiting room. Doctors had two waiting rooms: white and colored. We had only two dentists in town, and neither would see African American patients.

One of Amelia's children developed a tooth ache. A tooth ache might seem like no big deal, but one can die from an infected tooth if not treated. Evidently Amelia's family had tried to pull the tooth but without success. I went to my dentist and asked him to treat the child. He told me that if he allowed black people in his office, his white patients would all desert him. I asked him again as a personal favor, and I may have reminded him how bad my teeth were. Our family's dental bills probably made his car payment. He told me he would close his office at noon, putting an "out to lunch" sign on the front door, and if I would bring the child and his mother down the alley to his back door, he would treat him. We did that and the child recovered, but I wondered how many other African Americans had to suffer from untreated dental problems. Auburn had no hospital, so patients had to go to Opelika. The hospital admitted blacks, but they had to stay on a segregated floor.

Instead of going to Opelika some blacks went to Tuskegee to an all-black hospital. Amelia's teenage daughter became pregnant and was taken to Tuskegee. Amelia came to us and said her daughter had lost too much blood during delivery and the hospital wanted $50.00 or donated blood for each pint. Could we help? Your grandfather has "O" type blood and is therefore a universal donor, but he had just given all he was allowed to me. I also had a new baby (your mother Julie) and had also lost a great deal of blood Since we couldn't help with blood or money, John volunteered to go with Amelia to some beer joints and ask for blood donors. At one meeting place, three black men volunteered to give blood. A young white man was also in the establishment trying to organize a freedom march. Neither Auburn University nor the town itself was integrated and the white people wanted things to stay that way. Several young white men from the North had come to town and tried to organize marches and one had been shot. (He survived.) People thought of the freedom riders as "outside agitators." This particular white "outside agitator" jumped in the car and eagerly volunteered to go give blood. And so, the carload of four blacks and two whites went 13 miles down the road to Tuskegee. My husband said that for the first time in his life he was afraid of being shot. What if someone recognized the civil rights worker? "This should not be happening in America," he said. No one shot them and they were able to complete their humanitarian mission to give blood to the young girl.

Love, "Magra"

Dear Rachel,

While we lived in Alabama, Auburn University was integrated. Governor Wallace had threatened to "stand at the schoolhouse door" to prevent African Americans from entering. Troops were sent and federalized to protect minority rights. One black student, Authorine Lucy, had entered the year before we arrived, but she left, probably because of the mistreatment she received. Another student, Harold Franklin, was now ready to enter, so the campus was surrounded by troops. Only people who had legitimate business on campus could enter. Those of us who worked and studied on campus had special passes. Anyone without one could be arrested. One mentally ill African American woman was accustomed to wandering in the town.

People knew she was harmless, so they let her go where she pleased. One day Miss Mattie Lou, as she was called, decided to enter the campus. When ordered to halt, she didn't. It took four troopers to tackle her and get her to the police station, where they received a "tongue lashing" from Auburn police for manhandling and abusing "one of our finest black citizens." Miss Mattie Lou was allowed to wander once more.

While this situation at Auburn was going on, your mother Julie was born. One Sunday I asked your grandfather to take care of the boys while I went to his deserted office on campus to finish typing my dissertation for my degree. While in this totally deserted place, I began to lose large amounts of blood. My doctor was out of town and the only other doctor did not take new patients. I called the hospital in Opelika, hoping to get an ambulance, but they had no ambulance service. "Come on to the hospital," they said, but I had no transportation. I called home but John had no car. I had our only car but was in no condition to drive. He was able to get a neighbor's car and did get me to the hospital. Before he came, however, I called the town's only taxi, owned by an African American and only used by African Americans. He agreed to help me, even though he knew he could be arrested for driving on campus. He also was not sure how to find me because my building was not marked. Luckily, as John drove up, I was able to call this good man and tell him not to come. After I got to the hospital, they told me my baby had no heartbeat, but after they gave me oxygen, the heartbeat returned. So now we have Julie.

After we received our degrees, your grandfather and I moved to Minnesota to get his PhD. Just as I had discovered in Pittsburgh, things were not perfect for minorities there either, although somewhat better than in the South because at least schools and businesses were integrated. Residential areas-not so much. One of the neighbors in our apartment building had a fit because a black family moved in. People would notice our Alabama license plates and say, "We don't like them either."

"Don't like who?" I might ask (although I knew), and they would say, "That Governor Wallace has the right idea." More later.

Dear Rachel,

When we lived in Alabama, President Kennedy was shot. Martin Luther King was too. After we moved to Minnesota, Bobby Kennedy was shot. The Vietnam War was raging. Many students who normally would not have gone to college now enrolled to avoid being drafted. Many did not believe in the war. Martin Luther King did not. There was a shortage of university teachers, so I was hired to teach English, even though I only had a master's degree. We read the classics and philosophers and then wrote essays about them. I absolutely loved teaching college students but could not sign a contract for the next year because I didn't know how long we were going to stay in Minnesota. Your grandfather's degree depended on his ongoing research, and we did not know how long that would take.

I found a short-term position in the state school for mentally ill children. The reason I got the job was because I had become friends with the head of the school, an African American psychologist, and his wife. I met them at church (yes, we were integrated) where they were trying to enlist help for their son. The young boy was severely brain-injured, and because my sister was also brain-injured, I wanted to help. At that time there was a theory that a brain which didn't function could be made to re-program itself. If a child never learned to walk, you first taught him to crawl, and if he didn't talk, you bombarded him with language. This theory is no longer believed, but at the time it was taught in graduate courses. It required two people to move the child in swimming and crawling positions while at the same time using language. It went on for 8 or 10 hours a day, so volunteers were needed for two- hour blocks. Another lady from church was my partner one session per week but other volunteers kept the program going every day. As we moved the child, we told children's stories, said poems and nursery rhymes, and when we couldn't think of anything else would just repeat, "Steven is a good boy; Steven is a wonderful kid."

His muscles improved with the exercise, and perhaps he enjoyed the verbal stories and poems, but he did not learn to walk or talk, at least during the period I volunteered.

This African American family invited our family to Thanksgiving in their large home in downtown Minneapolis. They said they preferred to live in the inner city where their daughter, who was Julie's age, could see other people who looked like her. If they moved to the suburbs, everyone else was white. The wife and mother, Jackie, told me that people sometimes asked her if she wished she were white. "No", she said. Her father was a wealthy black doctor with lots of patients and her mother belonged to the highest social class in the black community. I think her hometown was St. Louis, and she told me that the black population was s very stratified by social class. Th highest class, to which she belonged, had elegant coming out parties for young girls and fancy balls. This couple also visited our house, which was very humble compared to theirs, an apartment in student housing. More later,

"Magra"

Dear Julie,

You may want to read these letters because some of the content may not be appropriate for Rachel's class. When I get started writing, I tend to tell the WHOLE story. I went to work for our friend, the black psychologist. My previous experience with African Americans was being THEIR boss. Now an African American was MY boss. I was forever sticking my foot in my mouth. I might say, "This child seems to be the black sheep of the family." Again, I might say, "That person has a black mark against his name." My boss would give me a dirty look and say, "And what is wrong with BLACK?" Fortunately, he had a sense of humor and might say, "Whatever possessed me to hire someone from Alabama?" The "BLACK IS BEAUTIFUL" movement had not yet caught on, but it was on the horizon. He did say that he would not normally hire someone who could not commit to a time period, but he had seen me working with his son and knew I would be good with atypical kids. And to be honest, most teachers did not want to work with the type of children we had.

The kids were divided into two groups: those who had committed crimes and those who were mentally ill but had not been in trouble with the law. I had only one African American student, a boy of nine or ten. He had been born to a white mother, but her family would not accept him, so he was given to a black family. He hated his adopted family and insisted he was really white. I gave him some stories of black heroes to read, hoping it might instill racial pride, but he refused. "I'm NOT like those people. I hate dirty. black____." I had another student who had killed his mother, but my job was not as hard as it might seem because we were allowed flexible schedules. I taught the child who wanted to abuse other students in a class all by himself. When the child who wanted to kick me in the shins was scheduled, I made sure to wear boots. They all had a tragic story, and were kept under lock and key, but I must say that this institution was a model environment. Students lived in cottages with married couples as their house parents. They were always clean and wearing nice clothing. They had good meals, psychological therapy and planned recreation. I worked in this school over 50 years ago and I think it was better run than most facilities for mentally ill children today. This is another area where civil rights are needed.

After John (your dad) received his PhD, we moved to Athens, Georgia, where he was hired by the University of Georgia. The schools were finally integrated, but there was turmoil. Michael and David were in the third grade and the first grade. They adjusted to integration, played sports with black boys, bringing some home to play after school. By the time David was in second grade, he had distinguished himself as the smartest student in math, so his African American teacher used him as a teaching assistant, giving him small groups to teach. You (Julie) went to a church kindergarten, as there was no kindergarten in public school, so you were well prepared to perform in first grade. However, the black children who had no opportunity to attend kindergarten, were woefully unprepared; many had no idea how to behave at school. You became very unhappy about going to school, not so much by how the children acted but how the teacher acted. She had a heavy hand with a paddle. When it was time to leave for school one morning, you went limp like a hippie protester, and I had to carry you into the school. I went to see the principal and told her that I thought the first-grade teacher was being too mean to the black children, and my daughter was so upset she didn't want to come to school. "I had to drag her into the building this morning," I said. The principal, who was handy with a paddle herself, said that students had to be disciplined and that my daughter was probably too sensitive. "I can't fire a teacher on the word of a child. Now if YOU saw something improper…"

I tried dropping into the classroom on one excuse or another but did not actually see the teacher abusing a child. And since she didn't do anything to MY child, the principal dismissed my complaint. Many white friends enrolled their children in private schools to avoid the turmoil of integration, but I was trying to be supportive of integration. Many years later Michael told me he was glad he had attended the integrated schools because he felt he could get along with "all types of people."

However, Michael had one experience as a high school senior that almost made him change his favorable attitude towards minorities. A prejudiced white boy in the school had been tormenting black students with racial slurs. To get revenge, some black students recruited adult friends and relatives to come to the school and beat up the white boy. The school scheduled some classes for 7 a.m., before most students arrived. As Michael pulled into the nearly deserted parking lot, he saw a group of black men and boys beating and stomping on a white boy on the pavement. He didn't like this white boy.

"He wasn't a special friend," Mike said, "but when I saw blood coming out of his mouth, I had to do something."

He rushed into the fray and began pulling the men and boys off their victim, but he was no match for them. They were too many. They beat him on the head until it was covered with knots. When I later ran my fingers over his scalp, it was lumpy, like a washboard. They had a board with a nail in it and scraped his chest and abdomen. He had a bloody scar but fortunately the nail did not puncture any organs. A female teacher arrived and ordered them to stop, but they slapped her and pushed her down. Finally, the police arrived. Michael did not go to school but fled to his girlfriend's house. (She was home with a cold.) John and I were at work so did not hear about the fight until we got home.

Several days later the principal announced that all students involved in this fight would be expelled. Mike's father (your dad) went to that principal's office and said, "My son may have saved that other boy's life. If you even think about expelling him and keeping him from graduation, you will have the biggest lawsuit you ever saw. And if you were doing your job, this might not have happened." Rumors had it that the principal had locked himself in the office when he heard of a potential race riot. This may not be true; it was a rumor. Michael graduated with honors soon after.

Dear Julie,

 Here again, some of this may not be appropriate for children. In Georgia I was hired by Follow Through, a federal program operating out of University of Georgia for the purpose of improving schools in poverty areas, including one in North Georgia, which was 95% white, and one in South Carolina, which was 95% black. Of all my careers, this one was the most rewarding, although not without its frustrations. I had never seen such poverty: people living in abandoned barns, living in cars, not getting medical attention, and literally starving. The families who had a shack to live in were the lucky ones. There was no free lunch at school until we got there. One little boy always carried home the milk we gave him "so I can feed my baby." One family had a set of twins in kindergarten but only sent one child at a time. I went to see this mother and asked why both children were not in school each day. "So, they can both eat," she said. Each boy was allowed to eat every other day. I explained that both children could eat every day if she would just send them to school. It seems they only had one pair of pants. One child wore them one day while the other stayed home naked, and then the other twin wore them the next day and was able to eat. We found her a pair of little boys' trousers. Needless to say, these kids were malnourished.

 In addition to free lunch, we started a clothing closet and put teachers' aides in the classrooms to help children who were so far behind in their subjects. Perhaps our best program was educating parents who had not completed high school. One of our first-grade students taught her mother to read. These parents who were interested could get a GED through our program and some even went on to get college degrees. If a mother completed two years of college, she could get a job working in classrooms, or perhaps distributing food and clothing to isolated families. This was a new source of income in the mountains. We also brought new books and teaching supplies into the classrooms. As our reading test scores went up, we were recognized as a model program. This does not mean that we were always well liked in the mountain program, mostly white. These people were fiercely independent and did not trust government.

 "We don't need no gov'ment help," they might say, or "We don't like people who come in from out." In other words, we should go home and mind our own business. Two situations helped us become more accepted. The program was run by a local doctor's wife who was beloved in the community. As a doctor's wife, she knew how many illnesses could be avoided by education and better nutrition. The people trusted her. The other situation evolved as more parents became educated themselves, they began to hope for a better life for their families and communities.

My other project, in South Carolina, was nearly all black. McCormick, the county seat, was run by the white power structure. The schools were not integrated until ordered by the "feds." Naturally, some people were not fond of anything related to federal government, but the person in charge, a respected upper class white lady, wanted to improve all schools, white and black. The McCormick schools were originally all white but a few blacks who lived near were allowed when integration was ordered. Most other blacks lived in two rural towns in the county. I was assigned to visit these all-black schools.

As I drove into these rural towns, I began to feel uneasy. I realized that I was the only white person within a radius of ten or twelve miles. Everything, not just the schools, was black-the stores, the small churches, everything was for blacks. I felt that I had always had good relations with black people, but now I began to think, "Maybe I'm not the right person for this job." To my relief, I was received warmly. The ladies who cooked in the cafeteria had even prepared a special meal "because we heard you were coming." Physically, the schools were a mess. There was no indoor bathroom. You had to go outside to some smelly privies. The teachers were forced to use cast-off books from the white school. The readers were all about those white kids, Dick and Jane. We brought in multi-cultural reading materials, plus science and math materials. Some of the teachers were mildly resentful because they did not want to change their methods, especially in the "new" math, but they were happy to get new reading materials, free lunches and teacher aides.

Some of the teachers began to use me as a "sounding board" to vent about all their frustrations against the white ruling class. Many of the men worked in a lumber mill. They did not get paid when it rained, and they hardly got paid when the sun shone. Their pay was so low that they were eligible for food stamps, but the bosses would not sign the papers which would enable them to get food. I went to see the boss man and he was hostile to me, claiming he didn't believe in "welfare handouts," but later he did start signing papers so workers could get help. The Federal government was demanding that there be no "all black" schools, so the white ruling class decided to raid an all-white orphans' home and sprinkle those children into the black schools. This plan was rightfully rejected. The government then had to agree that if there were no available white children, the schools could not be integrated. However, the staff must be integrated. A white minister's wife and two white college students, plus the daughter of our program director, agreed. None had teaching degrees, but they were dedicated. Thus, the schools were integrated.

I enjoyed my three years in this poverty program, Follow Through, because it met multiple needs of children and families. When teaching in a regular school, a teacher might think, "Johnny could do better if he had enough to eat, had more help with his schoolwork, had eye glasses, etc." In this program, these needs could be met, and Johnny did do better at school.

I had to leave my job because we were moving to Indiana. John became department head of the small animal clinic at Purdue. I could not find a job, so volunteered in Julie's second grade, where I helped a child learn to read. The principal of that school recommended me to another school where I taught first grade. First grade is rewarding because the children walk in the door not knowing how to read, and in the spring, they walk out the door (hopefully) knowing how to read. This school had only one disadvantage: no special education so special needs were not met. It also had no free breakfast or lunch, so I ended up feeding one little girl who was always hungry. In this school and in my children's schools there were no black students. We did have one black faculty member.

My students did well in reading and math, so the principal hired me for three years. He did have one complaint. I was not very good at group discipline, but it was not a huge problem because most of my students were well behaved. We moved back to Georgia so John could be Department Head in the College of Veterinary Medicine at University of Georgia. I did not go back to Follow Through because the program was winding down. The director had some health problems and had fired almost everyone I had known. The program was phased out several years later. It is ironic that whenever a program is doing good, it loses support. One exception is Head Start. It still exists.

I was hired by a public school to teach grades 1-3 in a combined class of 75 children. We had three teachers and two aides. One third of the class consisted of upper middle-class white children. A few had behavior problems but mostly they conformed to the rules. Another third of the class consisted of black children who had been to Head Start or some other preschool program. These children not only knew how to behave at school, but they outperformed their white peers on such tasks as knowing the alphabet and understanding numbers. The other 25% of the class, all black, came from a notorious housing project, known for its crime and drugs. These children ended my career at this school. One of my teaching partners was a charismatic black teacher who used her paddle only in extreme cases. The children could relate to her because she was "like" them. The other partner was a middle-aged white woman, who had lots of teaching experience and a paddle, which she used frequently. In addition, our special education children had not been diagnosed yet. (Children usually did not get put into special classes until about third grade.) We had several children who were so mentally ill that they screamed and fought constantly. In my group there was a boy who was sweet but supposedly dying of kidney disease. It became my responsibility to take him in the boys' rest room every hour and check his catheter. If he had blood in his urine, I was to call for emergency help. While I was doing this, the other children I was supposed to be watching might be flooding the bathroom.

Whenever I thought about using the paddle, I had visions of white people beating black slaves. I remembered my daughter's first grade teacher who traumatized not only the children she hit but those who witnessed these beatings. I did not want to be like her. I resigned before I could be fired. I did not blame my teaching peers. They tried to help me. Most who paddled justified their behavior, "It's the kind of discipline they get at home, so it's all they understand." Even one professor I consulted, said I should hit them, "but not too hard."

"If they won't shut up and sit down and listen to the lesson, they will never learn to read, and then they will be doomed to a life of poverty and crime," he said. I consulted another professor,

Dr. Adeline Barber, who had been my wonderful boss at Follow Through. She wisely said, "If keeping your job means doing something you feel is wrong, then it is not worth it."

Although Dr. Barber's advice helped me feel a little better, I still felt terrible about myself. I had spent years of my life trying to make things better for blacks and impoverished whites, but now my career and reputation were ruined because I couldn't control unruly black children. I felt like a total failure, yet I did know two facts: I DID know how to teach reading, and I DID NOT dislike black children. To reassure myself, I started a free summer school in my home for children who had failed first or second grade We had 26, about two thirds of them black. They came in morning and afternoon groups, so we were not overwhelmed. We did fun activities, like baking cookies and reading the recipes, playing word games, and reading children's stories. My own children helped them read. There was not a single discipline problem, although most were very poor. Several children who previously had not read a word started reading. It was a joy to see their faces when they realized they could read. Most improved their reading test scores.

I had been taking graduate courses toward a doctorate, so I was able to finish my degree and get a job teaching at a small college, now Piedmont University. It was a pleasant interlude; the faculty was friendly and college students don't throw erasers. Unfortunately, the drive was too long, and the pay was even less than what I could make in public school. Our own children were entering college, so I wanted more pay. I briefly accepted an English position in a rural high school, mostly white, and learned an unpleasant lesson: unruly white students can be just as bad as unruly blacks. And I was no good at controlling either type. Four of my classes had mostly sweet students but one was called by other teachers as "the class from hell." They did things like set fires in the classroom, and they bragged to me that their last teacher had to go to a "mental home." I checked with other teachers and found it was true: the students had given her a "nervous breakdown." I didn't want to have one so ended up in another school closer to home teaching gifted students. I have to admit that they fired me on the way out the door, the only time I have actually been fired. The school with the 75 children in the class might have done so, had I not left voluntarily.

I had to admit that the fault was mine. I am conflict phobic. I don't like unpleasant conflict. It may have originated in childhood when our father urged us to "agree with whatever our mother wanted us to do" so she wouldn't be upset and have a "spell." We didn't stand up for ourselves. I also had mixed feelings about corporal punishment. I was against it in schools but sometimes spanked our kids at home. My former boss, Dr. Barber, said she sometimes did the same." My kids know I love them when I discipline them, but we don't always know if the teachers love them," she said. My own mother said she disapproved of any adult hitting any child, but she occasionally got angry and hit us. Then she felt guilty and berated herself for doing what she felt was wrong. I have found that in schools where spanking is the main form of discipline, both in the classroom and in the office, a teacher who doesn't use this discipline has a hard time surviving. Some children will "walk all over" the teacher and then wipe their feet on him/her. Today spanking is illegal in many states. It is still legal in Georgia, but most schools no longer condone corporal punishment.

Although I spanked our children on occasion, none of our children use that method of discipline on their own children. Conservative pundits say, "that's what is wrong with today's kids," but my grandchildren have never been discipline problems, and the research now suggests what while spanking may stop bad behavior temporarily, the long-term effects are negative. Times have changed. When I was growing up, a parent who did not spank was not a "good mother "(or father).

Back to the topic of my conflict phobia, the cause did not matter. This was the root of some of my discipline problems. I needed to fix myself. I enrolled in a class called "How to be More Assertive." No grades were given, which was a good thing, or I probably would have made "F." One of our assignments was taking spoiled meat back to the store and demanding a refund. Another assignment was called the "Broken Record." You kept repeating the same request or demand until you got what you wanted. Donald Trump must have taken this class. Although being assertive is not the same as being aggressive, it didn't feel like "me." So much for self- improvement.

What does my personality have to do with civil rights? In Alabama in the 60's I justified not marching for civil rights. John and I had small children and we didn't need to get ourselves killed, (although he could have been shot just driving a carload of blacks to the hospital). I also hated the violence that resulted from these "non-violent" marches. One of my neighbors said, "Martin Luther King may be non-violent, but violence always follows his marches." She was blaming non-violent black people for the violence of white people.

Years later we lived in Georgia, and I was working for Follow Through. As previously noted, I had one project site which was nearly all white and another site which was nearly all black. The teachers liked to visit between projects to see what the others were doing in the classroom. Whenever I was driving a carload of blacks through certain counties, we had to keep a low profile. We didn't dare stop, even for a hamburger. Forsyth County and Dawson County had a reputation for "No blacks after sundown." My teachers and I couldn't trust them in the daytime either.

Eventually a black family had the audacity to move to Forsyth County. Of course, they were abused, so civil rights activists decided to get involved. Martin Luther King had been dead for years, but Hosea Williams and John Lewis were alive. I am sure Hosea Williams was there. Busloads of blacks arrived, as well as politicians from the Democratic party. The Ku Klux Klan was there. In spite of being a coward, I decided to join the march.

We had a rare snow, and the town was ghostly white as we marched around the town square. As expected, "our side" was mostly black and "their side" was mostly white. My partner was a young black woman who said, "Will you help me if those bad people come after me?"

I answered, "I'm not sure what I could do," and she replied, "You could cover me up with snow, so they would think I was white." She was trying to make a joke to cover up fear. The white protesters stood on the sidelines yelling insults: "N-lovers, go home." One said to me, "How many N-s did you F- today?" They did not shoot us, but they pelted us with snowballs. As I was going to my car, I was confronted by three Klans people, dressed in their white robes and silly pointy hoods. They said some filthy things to me, but then one of them, a young blonde came closer to me and said, "I'm curious. We all know that N's are dirty, evil people but you look like a respectable white lady. Why would you want to march with them?" I noticed she had a gold cross at her neck. I pointed to it and said, "because Jesus said to love everybody, even you." They went away.

The next question is: did I march for Black Lives Matter? The answer is "no." I am nearly eighty-five and it is all I can do to walk to the mailbox. John has to use a walker. Some of our children and grandchildren marched, and I am proud of them. Nevertheless, I am not happy with how some of these marches have deteriorated into hedonism and violence. Some of my liberal friends might argue that I care more about "a few broken windows" than the lives of black people. Of course, I care about the lives of black people, but as the wonderful African American mayor of Atlanta has said to the people tearing up her city, "You are not honoring anybody by running down the street with stolen liquor." Some of the statues they have torn down include Abraham Lincoln and Ulysses Grant, two people who ended slavery. When Martin Luther King marched, his people sang hymns and he spoke scripture and used other language to appeal to our better angels. Today's extremists, both far left and far right, have a very limited vocabulary. The only word they know is the "F" word.

I admit that there is a pervasive culture of racism in some police departments that needs to be rooted out. The black men who were killed by police expose a tragic pattern. Some police are prejudiced against all minorities. One of our Hispanic friends was abused and taken to jail because of a minor traffic violation. But if someone is breaking into my home with a gun, I don't want them to send a social worker. I agree that social workers should accompany police on all mental health calls, but I do not believe in "defunding the police." They need more money, not less, if they are going to pay social workers and pay higher salaries to attract and train high-quality police officers, those men and women who risk their lives to protect us.

I also remember that Martin Luther King, in his Letter from the Birmingham Jail said that moderates (like me) are worse than the Klan. I also have seen signs saying that "Silence is violence," so I will try to be more "woke" by voting and contributing to candidates who support racial justice.

Love, Mom P a g e | 35

III. SEX: "ME TOO" in 1954

Almost every day we hear of another woman coming forth to reveal a "Me too "experience of sexual abuse. The parameters of the term have expanded to include incidents of hugging, kissing, or just, "He put his hand on my back." We all have different definitions and preferences about personal space, but I frequently get hugged and kissed when I walk into church. The difference is mainly age-I am 84 years old. Most of my "huggers are over 75, although occasionally I get a hug from a younger person whom I might have taught in school or Sunday School. And then there's family: we have three children, two daughters-in-law and 10 grandchildren. We hug and kiss.

While I think that a few people have cried "sexual abuse" about minor touching incidents, I do not mean to diminish the pain of those who were truly abused sexually. I am sympathetic because it happened to me when I was 16. But times were different then. The victim was always, always blamed.

In high school, one of my best friends, whom I will call "Jan," had a brother who was involved in an attempted gang rape. A carload of boys picked up a girl of "questionable reputation", took her to an empty parking lot and attempted rape. I don't know if any of them succeeded, but she broke free, escaped from the car and ran, half naked, to a movie theater; the police were called, the boys were arrested, but no harsh punishment followed. Counseling was recommended. The boys escaped punishment because they were able to claim that the girl had a bad reputation. In those days, any girl who had sex without marriage, especially if she had sex with more than one person, was branded a "whore" and therefore deserved any treatment she received.

Although no jail time was served by Jan's brother, some of her friends deserted her because of what her brother did. She had planned a slumber party for 10 girls but only one other girl besides me came. The other girls' parents had said, "If you go to that house and that brother is there, you might be attacked." My parents were normally over-protective, but they hadn't heard about Jan's brother. We three girls celebrated Jan's birthday. Her brother was probably restricted to his room because he never showed his face.

During this same period of time another sex scandal circulated in the rumor mill. A former graduate from our school, whom I'll call Thad, had gone to work at a chemical plant where a horrible fire had almost killed him. He wasn't supposed to live but he survived, with a gruesome face that was almost melted. One ear was even burned off. Once recovered, he went out with a girl, who may have felt sorry for him, but she had run away claiming that he tried to rape her. This time the case did come to court, but it was determined that he was only trying to kiss her, and his burned face had made her panic and run away. In the court of public opinion, some believed in his innocence, but others whispered that he might be dangerous. His younger brother, whom I'll call Don, a quiet and seemingly well-behaved boy, became the object of crude jokes and shaming because of his brother. My friend Jan decided to be kind to Don, because she knew how it felt to be shamed for what a family member did. I also had some empathy for Don because I was sometimes shamed for having a sister who was brain injured. "Your sister is a retard," they might taunt.

I was moderately surprised when Don asked me to go to a church picnic on a Sunday afternoon. I already had a boyfriend at Texas A &M (my current husband of 63 years), but I thought, "I'll just go with Don to that picnic as a friend." After I had agreed to go, Don told me, "Jan is going with my brother."

If we had had cell phones in those days, I would have texted, "What R U thinking? R U out of your mind?" This was not a time of instant communication. Jan later told me she thought I was the one who had lost my mind.

It wasn't until we were in the car that I realized that I was supposed to be with Thad, the notorious brother. I briefly considered pretending to be sick, but then I thought, "It's a public park with a crowd of church people. If I stay around others, I will be OK."

After we ate our picnic lunch, Don and Jan decided to take a walk. Thad suggested we do the same, but I said, "I don't want to take a walk (in the woods.) "I would rather sit here at the picnic table and talk." And so, we did. He told me about his accident and how being near death made him want to do something better with his life. He was planning on being a minister and serving God. He also entertained me with magic tricks and told me he used his hobby of magic to entertain patients in burn units. He told me he liked to entertain children recovering from burns in the hospital and encourage them that they could get well. I could not help thinking, "What a really nice guy," although I had a fleeting thought that, because of his face, he might frighten the children in the burn units.

He did not make any sexual advances, and when we returned, he asked if he could see m*e* again. I told him I had a boyfriend in college, but if he wanted to talk, we could talk on the phone. I would be his friend, but no dating.

He did call-several times a week. We talked about a variety of subjects, mostly religion because he belonged to a different tradition than I did. I also had the same English teacher that he had had in high school, so we talked about English literature. He nearly always ended with a plea to go out, promising to be "just friends".

Our mutual high school English teacher had been somewhat of a mentor to me; I considered her wise, so I went to see her and asked what she knew about Thad, her former student. She said he was very smart and one of her best students. He had also been handsome and popular before he was burned.

She told me he had been in love with a band majorette, but the girl rejected him after the accident. "That may be why he is attracted to you," she said. I was also a band majorette. Her advice for me was to be kind from a distance. She did not really believe he was capable of rape, but she said, "That tragic accident may have made him crazy, so don't go off alone with him."

As fall arrived, Thad was preparing to go away to college. "I want to see you just one time before I leave," he begged. Because there was a movie at the neighborhood theater that we both wanted to see, I gave in. My dad had a habit of lecturing my dates: "I know that movie is over at 10:27 and you can have 20 minutes to get something to drink, so you better have her back here at 10:52." He allowed five minutes for driving after the drink. My parents also had a rule that I could not go out with anybody older than my brother (about three years), Thad was actually a year older than my brother, but when asked, I said, "He's the same age." My parents also would never had made remarks about how ugly this young man was. Our family, because of my sister's handicap, believed in being kind to those with disabilities.

Once in the car, Thad bragged about his new ear, swaddled in white gauze. A plastic surgeon had made it for him and was planning to do some more work on his face. I was happy he had a new ear, but then he said, "We aren't going to a movie." I began to have bad vibes as he drove to a bar, but I didn't know how to protest. I was under 18 and did not patronize bars, but then I thought, "At least we are not alone. "I had been afraid he might take me to some deserted place. Inside, I realized that we must be in a gay bar. I knew very little about gay people, but I saw that all the clients were male-and some called Thad by name. He ordered alcohol but I stayed with a soft drink. If I got arrested for being in a bar, I didn't want to get charged with under-age drinking. The only pleasant part of this awful evening was the music. A very talented pianist played the haunting melody of Malaguena.

In spite of the beautiful music, I told Thad I was uncomfortable and wanted to go home. To my surprise, he agreed, even though he hadn't finished his drink. To my relief, he seemed to be driving home, but when we came to a fork in the road, left to home and right into a pine forest, he turned right.

"You made the wrong turn," I gasped, "You should have gone left."

"I know what I am doing," was his steely reply.

I panicked. "It's true," I thought, "All those rumors. He really is a dangerous person." I decided to open the door and run as soon as we stopped, but as I looked around, there were only acres of pine trees. I would never make it back to the dim lights on the main road. I didn't really have time to decide on running because he literally pounced on me. He pushed me down and was on top of me; his mouth covered mine and his nose pressed against mine so that I could not breathe. His hands seemed to be choking my neck. My hands were pinned underneath. He ripped off the front of my dress. How could he do that and choke me at the same time? But he did.

"I'm going to die like Desdemona," I thought. Our English class had been studying Shakespeare, and the teacher had let us watch an old film of Othello. In the movie Othello believed that his wife, Desdemona, had cheated, so he covered her face with a scarf and then kissed her to death, smothering her and cutting off her air. Only as he walked in her funeral procession did Othello learn the truth. Desdemona had never cheated. I must have lost consciousness for several minutes before I realized that I could breathe. His face was no longer pressing on mine and his hands were not choking my neck, but he was doing something indecent under my skirt. I was able to get an arm free and whack him on the side of the head. I hit his new ear and the blood began to stain the bandage.

"Now I've done it," I thought," he will surely kill me." But he didn't.

Instead of attacking me again, Thad began to apologize profusely, "I'm sorry, I don't know what came over me. I would never want to hurt you," He became a totally different person.

I had the good sense to speak soothing lies, "I'm OK. It's all right." But then I said, "We'd better get home before my father comes looking."

To my relief, he started the motor and drove back to the road, this time turning left to my house. He was still apologizing when we reached my door. His personality change was so abrupt that if I were his therapist today, I might think he had DID, sometimes called multiple personality disorder.

Getting out of the car, I tucked the top of my dress into my bra and held the side seams together by pressing my upper arms tightly against my sides. I prayed my parents would not be up. Luckily, they were already in bed. "You're late," my dad called from the back bedroom, but because it was only a few minutes, they didn't get up or say any more. I slipped out of the torn dress, rolled it into a ball, and hid it in the bottom of my closet. The next day I sewed it up, and months later, when it fell apart in the wash, my mother and I agreed that today's clothes were cheaply made.

Today when we hear of sexual misconduct, we wonder, "Why did she wait so long to tell?" We might also wonder, "If her boss abused her, why did she go back to work?" If a friend or acquaintance was to blame, we wonder, "Why did she continue to associate with that person?"

I will try to explain based on what happened to me: it was a different culture. Parents and teachers ruled by guilt. My parents were not unusual; many of my friends had parents who could induce guilt. A friend's mother once stopped me after church. "Honey", she asked,"are you sure you are a Christian? Because you've been wearing too much lipstick."

What might have happened if my parents had found out? Probably my father would have gone after Thad with a gun. He had already threatened a mentally ill neighbor who accidentally walked into our house and caught my mother half dressed. My mother, on the other hand, might have said, "It was your fault because you lied." It was true; I had not been entirely honest about Thad's age.

If other people in the community found out, they might say, " Maybe her dress was too low," (It was modest by today's standards.) Or they might even observe, "Isn't she that band majorette who prances around the football field in a short skirt?" I did not want anyone to know what happened, although much later I told a couple of close friends.

Some people who are sexually assaulted feel that their lives are ruined forever. In my case, this didn't happen I earned college degrees and have a good marriage and wonderful children and grandchildren. However, there were some psychological effects: a combination of guilt and fear. I felt guilt that I had been so stupid to ignore my teacher's advice about being alone with Thad. Maybe guilt can explain why I went to his church two days later. I also felt irrational guilt that I may have ruined his plastic surgery by whacking his ear.

The attack happened on Friday. On Saturday he called "to make sure we are good." I gave some sort of neutral response. Then he asked me to come to his church the next day and have lunch with his parents. To this day, I don't fully understand why I agreed, but the next morning I slid into a pew beside him and his parents. I was relieved to see that his plastic ear was still on his head and covered with a clean bandage-no blood.

I don't remember what the minister said or even what his parents looked like. I do remember eating roast beef and listening to his parents talk about how they loved to play Santa at Christmas for their two boys. "One year we bought bikes, but they found them before Christmas and ruined the surprise," they told me. It seemed to me that they were trying to convince me (and perhaps themselves) that they were good parents in spite of what might have happened later.

After this day I never accepted another invitation to see Thad. Because he still had a few days before leaving for college, he wanted to see me again.

"I will never go out with you again," I told him.

"But I thought you forgave me; you came to my church…"

"I did forgive you, but I am afraid of you…" In my faith tradition, if we do not forgive, we will go to hell.

" But I promised to never do that again…"

"You told me you couldn't help what you did, so how can you promise?"

I had a part time job at a tearoom in a department store. In the 1950's women wore hats and gloves and fancy dresses to go shopping. They might visit a beautiful tearoom for lunch. I miss those days. My job was to be hostess, seating the guests and passing out menus. I also helped at the cash register. The walls next to the stairway leading down into the tearoom were covered in mirrors. I looked up, and to my dismay, saw Thad's face reflected in all those mirrors. He could not see me yet, so I asked a waitress to cover for me and fled to the kitchen, and once in the kitchen, I crouched down besides huge pots and pans.

On earlier occasions, Thad had offered to pick me up at work "so you won't have to ride the bus." I always declined. My boss was not happy to see me cowering in the kitchen instead of doing my job, but when

I told her I was being stalked, she let me stay there until we were sure he was gone.

I went away to college and did not hear from Thad for three years. He went to a different college, but unbeknownst to me, he was expelled for starting a fire. (Why are we not surprised that he was obsessed with fire?) He somehow landed on my campus. I saw him in a crowd across the street and hurried to my class. I had hoped he didn't see me, but in the evening, he called, acting as though we were long-lost friends.

"We must meet for coffee."

"Never, absolutely not."

"I will get even, you little bitch."

When I hung up the phone, my roommate looked at it with disgust and grabbed a towel to wipe it dry. My palms were dripping wet with sweat. I was feeling intense fear, even after three years.

I managed to avoid Thad until I graduated, but I did run into a high school friend who had recently transferred to my college. She told me she had seen Thad and gone out with him, and he had tried to rape her. It was a "Me too" moment.

"Did he try to choke you?" I asked.

"Yes," she replied.

This girl was braver than I had been. She complained to authorities, but nothing was ever done.

After graduation, I was at an alumni meeting, and when one woman found out where I was from, she asked if I knew Thad. "I was a bridesmaid in his wedding," she said. "But he got me into a secluded area at one of the parties and tried to be sexual."

"Did you tell the bride?" I asked. "Yes, but she married him anyway."

He was now a minister and also married to the daughter of a minister.

Some fifty years later and many miles away, I received a phone call from Don, Thad's brother. Although I had attended several reunions. I had never seen either of the brothers. Thad, of course, was four years older. Don told me he was part of a small group from our old high school friends who remained close. They wanted to get together more often than reunions provided. Yes, Facebook had been invented, but these friends wanted more personal contact. Would I like to be a part of the group?

"I can't be friends with you, Don, because of your brother. I had an unfortunate experience with Thad, and if I share details of my life with you, he might find out and use the information to do me harm."

Was I wrong to be unkind to Don? Could he be blamed for what his brother was or is? Would I want to be blamed for things my brother might have done? But then I remembered that it was Don who tricked me into meeting his brother.

Thad had actually tried to reach me on social media (not Facebook). I not only deleted but got off that site. I stayed off Facebook and resisted other sites, too. And when I hung up the phone from Don, my palms were sweaty.

It has now been 66 years since my traumatic encounter. I assume Thad is dead. Why tell the story now? As I read, or hear in the media, some of the "Me-too" stories, I also hear people responding, 'Why did she wait so long to tell?" I know why. But sometimes I might also feel that some women could be over-reacting to a friendly hug or touch from a male. Perhaps there is a reason a woman might over-react to a friendly, innocent touch: she may have been abused earlier. What I do know is this: every case is different.

I had one other bad experience related to "Me too." I had a scholarship to the University of Pittsburgh, and though I still had a boyfriend in Texas, we had agreed that we should date others. I accepted a double date to some college function, and after the event the driver in the front seat drove to a nearby park. The couple in the front seat started kissing. My date wanted to do more than kissing. He even had the nerve to ask, "What do I have to do to get some? Go steady with you? I'll do it."

"No, you won't." I said I wanted to go home. The driver in the front seat knew I meant business, so he took me back to my boarding house.

The two boys belonged to a fraternity which had a large dinner bell in the yard. If a fraternity brother had been able to "score" with a date, he rang the bell and his brothers congratulated him on his "home run." My date rang the bell.

About this time, I received a letter from the college informing me that I was receiving a Mortar board Award for good grades (and the assumption of good character.) The Mortar Board Society was for seniors, but they gave awards to lower classes. This was spring semester, and the sororities were having delayed rush. I had been invited to four sororities and also had a 3.7 grade average. I felt really good about how my life was going and wrote a letter to my parents about the Mortar Board award.

After the date which ended badly, my date kept calling, and when I refused him, he had his friends call to tell me that I should forgive him and give him a second chance. Some of the other fraternity brothers who believed that the ringing bell was actually the truth called and said I should date them.

We had one wall pay phone for 12 girls in the house. It was outside the housemother's door, and she probably heard every word. I asked this housemother to please refuse any calls from boys, and of course she wanted to know why. This sixty-year-old woman had once been a prison guard, and she now perceived her duty as protecting the morals of her girls. The housemother contacted the dean of women (so the dean would know she was doing her job of protecting our morals.) The dean was a person who believed, "If there is smoke, there must be fire." In other words, if too many boys were calling, I must be guilty of something.

On the day of the Awards Ceremony, I eagerly awaited to be called to the stage for my Mortar Board Award. When they came to that place in the program, they skipped over it to the next award. I thought, "Maybe they just rearranged the order of events and will call me at the end." They didn't. No Mortar Board Award for me.

Two of the four sororities who had invited me withdrew their invitations, citing lame excuses. Luckily, the two who still wanted me were my favorites. I had good friends in the one I joined and they knew my character. My big sister in the sorority said I should fight the Mortar Board affair, but I did not want further notoriety. I had already written my parents I was getting the award. Happily, they lived too far away to attend the ceremony, so they never found out.

Sexual abuse can be physical, such as rape or beating and choking, or it can affect the heart and mind because of lies and rumors. I survived both. Healing is possible.

IV. CONCLUSION

After living in Indiana, we returned to Georgia and have remained here 45 years. John served as department head of the Small Animal Clinic at the University of Georgia. Upon retiring, he taught animal neurology and mentored doctoral students. At one point he was named Teacher of the Year. He helped found a veterinary professional organization, the American College of Veterinary Internal Medicine Association and was awarded the Robert W. Kirk Distinguished Service Award. One year we traveled to Texas A&M where he received the Distinguished Alumnae Award. As mentioned earlier, he wrote two textbooks on animal neurology and numerous articles and chapters in other texts.

After we moved to Georgia the second time, I finished my doctorate and taught college two years, then went back to public school. The principal wanted me to teach gifted education. The whole idea was ironic because my own IQ would not have qualified me to be in that program. The cut off was 130, but allowing for statistical variance of 2 points, a child with a score of 128 could get in. I might have been accepted under this criterion.

I have said that working for Follow Through at UGA was my favorite job, but gifted education was probably my second favorite. Smart children are fun. Some parents have said to me, "I don't want my child to be gifted. I just want her to be normal." However, gifted children are usually better adjusted socially than those with less ability.

Other teachers did not want me to pull the brightest students from their classes, and they worried, rightly so, that the students would miss what they were teaching. We finally solved the problem (almost) by pulling children from science and social studies. Many teachers neglected these subjects anyway; they preferred to concentrate on math and reading, which would show up on test scores. I promised to cover the science and social studies texts the teachers were using, and because these children could read faster, we still had time for creative activities. For science, we collected rain from all over the world, including our own neighborhoods, and tested it chemically for acid rain. Acid rain was big news at that time. With my husband's help, we visited the veterinary school and even watched surgery. We also went to Huntsville, Alabama, to learn about training of astronauts. We went to Cape Kennedy in Florida and were taught by a real rocket scientist.

For social studies, we visited the World's Fair in Knoxville, Tennessee, to learn about the world's cultures. We also visited Epcot Center in Florida and filled out workbooks on each country. I was a counselor for an organization called Youth for Understanding. We had foreign students staying in our home, so we had them visit my classes to talk about their countries. At the University of Georgia was a professor, Dr. Paul Torrance, who taught creative thinking. His wife taught our children a method of creative problem solving. We went to the state contest for problem solving and won third place.

After I worked with gifted children for six years, the state decided to save money and raise the bar for eligible children. They now had to have an IQ of 135. Over half of my students had scores between 128 and 135. These students were told they could no longer participate. It was hard to explain to parents that "your child was gifted last year but now she isn't." There were many disgruntled parents. Although providing enrichment for gifted students seems like a good idea, the actual implementation is difficult. The schools finally decided to have teachers of gifted work in the classrooms with regular teachers to provide enrichment. For me this was less rewarding; I felt like just a teacher aide, so went back to remedial reading and stayed in this position for 10 years. Remedial teaching was rewarding because most of the children improved, but some children could not improve because of emotional problems. When I told the class to "have a nice Thanksgiving," one little girl threw her chair. "How can I have a nice Thanksgiving when my mama is in jail?" Her mama had offered a neighbor sex with the child in exchange for drugs. The little girl told and the mama and neighbor were sent to jail where they belonged. Sadly, her relatives told the child that it was all her fault.

Most of these disturbed children had a single mother who was either mentally ill, on drugs or addicted to alcohol, sometimes all three. Many did not know who their fathers were. One little boy would come to school at 3 a.m. to escape the turmoil in his home. He had two brothers whose father was somewhat involved, but he did not know who his father was. His complexion was darker than the brothers, so his mentally ill mother told him he could not eat because "he was too black." This child was fed at school, but I found myself bringing him snacks. He asked me to adopt him, and though I loved him, John and I felt we were too old (in our sixties) at this stage of our lives. There were many children with problems, some homeless, some living in cars. Social services were involved, but they told me and our teachers to stop referring so many children because "they had no place to put them." Two of my children died of neglect after I had already written reports on them. I studied and got a license in counseling so I could help these children.

After retiring from public school, I worked as counselor at our local Catholic School and also a counseling agency. There has been a lot of debate about the merits of private schools versus public. I think both are good, but public schools are usually better for the child with special needs. Private schools usually cater to the average or slightly above average child. Some very bright students told me they transferred out of private school because the public school offered a more challenging curriculum. Most public schools seem to offer more for the child who is below average but also for the child who is intellectually gifted. What about funding? If too much money is drained from public schools, then they become the "places of last resort." I was a local president of the Georgia Association of Educators, sometimes referred to as the "teachers' union", and their position was all for public education. I also belong to Phi Delta Kappa, a professional organization all about improving education for all. Nevertheless, I believe that not all children are alike and private schools may be the answer for some children, especially for those who want religious education. I would not object to a small amount of government money to fund scholarships for private education. Personally, I enjoyed working in the Catholic school because they promoted Christian values.

Our children all graduated from Cedar Shoals (public) High School: Michael in 1978, David in 1981, and Julie in 1983. Julie was valedictorian, one of five girls who had perfect grade point averages. Michael went to Auburn University and became a reporter and then an editor, first at the Birmingham News, then at the Orlando Sentinel, then at the Oakland Tribune, and finally returning to Birmingham, where he got his start.

In spite of what you may have heard, journalism is an honorable and necessary profession in a democracy. In Russia they poison journalists who disagree with the government, in Saudi Arabia (or Turkey) they kill unpopular journalists and cut them into pieces, in the middle east they might behead them or burn them alive. In California a journalist was shot for exposing gang activity; our son and his reporter exposed this killer who was then caught and punished. Michael, who now has a fatal disease, has done so much good: going into a prison riot to negotiate surrender, exposing fake charities who stole peoples' money, writing touching human- interest stories, and more. Now that he is afflicted with Lewy Body disease, he has raised thousands of dollars to support the Lewy Body Dementia Association in Lithonia, Georgia, and research at the University of Alabama at Birmingham. For a while Michael was unable to write, but his brother David has connected him with a doctor at Cleveland Clinic, who prescribed a new medicine. The medicine has almost eliminated his violent hallucinations, and he is writing again. Look for Mike Oliver at AL.com, entitled MyVinylCountdown.com. He specializes in music reviews.

It hurts me to hear our former president and those who admire him talk about the "lying media." As if they were all one voice. Some writers do lean to the left, but others lean to the right. I try to read and listen to all sides, even Fox News upon occasion. News reporting is necessary in a free society, which is why dictators try to eliminate or discredit most media.

Michael married Catherine, his childhood sweetheart, who became a Presbyterian pastor. They have three daughters who all live in Birmingham. Hannah is a teacher, Emily works with computers, and Claire is an occupational therapist. Hannah is married to Tom, a college teacher, and Claire is married to Ramsey, a journalist like her father. Ramsey' father, John Archibald, is also a journalist and a guest teacher at Harvard, His new book, Shaking the Gates of Hell, will be published in March.

David graduated from Georgia Tech, majoring in Industrial Management, and became a successful realtor. He specializes in commercial real estate, developing shopping centers, many in or near Hilton Head Island. His wife, Lori, a University of Georgia graduate, specializes in public relations, helping other businesses become successful. She also has her own business, developing new products. Their oldest son, Zack, graduated from the University of Maryland and is a media journalist for CNN in Washington DC. He recently was "too close for comfort" to the capitol riots. Their daughter, Alex, graduated from the University of Georgia, then went to medical school in Augusta. Soon she will officially be an M.D. and will likely specialize in pediatrics. The youngest son, Joe, has a business degree from Georgia Tech and works for the Atlanta Hawks.

Julie graduated from the University of Georgia with a degree in International business and then worked for Disney in Orlando, Florida.

When she first applied at Disney, they told her that they were not interested; they had too many applicants. However, when hey met her, they decided "she had a "Disney face." She laughed and wondered if they thought she looked like Daisy Duck or Minnie Mouse. Before she graduated from college, she took classes in Holland and in France. Because she knew French, she considered going to France when Disney opened a theme park there, but then she married a Canadian medical student. He later became well-known in the profession and is the head of a hospital in Colorado. They were married 30 years and had two sons and two adopted Vietnamese daughters.

The oldest son, Jake, has a degree in engineering from Colorado and a masters' in environmental design from a university in Vancouver, Canada. He is Canadian, having been born there, and hopes to design cities more friendly to the environment. His career has been paused, due to the pandemic, but I am confident he will succeed. The second son, Graeme, graduated from the University of Washington., where he published a research paper on reducing nitrogen in the atmosphere and is looking for graduate programs to fit his science interests. Both of these grandsons seem intent on helping the environment. Sophie, the oldest Vietnamese granddaughter, is a scholarship student at Pace University in New York. Her sister Rachel, still in middle school, lives with her mother Julie in Portland, Oregon.

When Julie married the Canadian medical student, they had no income, and she was not legally permitted to work in Canada. She worked undocumented as a waitress in order to put food on their table, so now she has some sympathy for our so-called "illegal aliens." She knows how they feel. Because she was married to a Canadian, she was eventually granted permission to work and she also earned an MBA. She became involved in the business aspects of upscale hotels, mainly the Canadian Pacific Hotel in Vancouver, where her husband was a medical resident. After moving to Boston, then to Chapel Hill, North Carolina, and finally to Portland, Oregon, she developed her own company, Well-Assembled Meetings, which arranged all the details for doctors' groups and other professional groups to hold conventions and earn the education hours they needed to keep professional licenses. In Portland, Oregon, newly divorced, she had booked over 50 meetings in 2019 and received some sort of award for her good planning. Then in 2020 the pandemic hit, and her business was almost destroyed. No one went to in-person meetings, so hotel rooms, meeting venues and food services all had to be cancelled. However, she was able to plan virtual meetings for those needing education hours, so gradually her business is creeping back.

Although we are proud of the children's and grandchildren's accomplishments, we are proudest of their character: all are good people, meaning they care about others. Throughout the years David and Lori bought bicycles for underprivileged children through their church; they taught their children to make pies for the homeless shelter; Lori was a Girl Scout leader and she and Alex were heavily involved in girls' clubs helping underserved girls. More recently, after Mike's terrible diagnosis, David and Lori have been a rock of support for his family, connecting them to resources such as the Cleveland Clinic; they have also given help and emotional support to Mike's three daughters, who are devastated by the turn of events in their family. I have already discussed Mike's good deeds, and his wife, Catherine, has also helped many people, including the homeless, when she was a pastor. She also has been extremely kind to my sister Jean. Over the years, Julie has supported World Vision, a Christian organization supporting children and their families around the world. One year, her son Graeme, said he wanted to give some family a goat instead of getting toys for Christmas. Each year I give some family a goat and chickens in honor of our grandson's unselfishness. Julie also has a project which helps diabetes patients; one year they were able to get 500 special shoes for patients who could not afford the right kind of shoes. Over the years she has done many things to help people; most recently she took food to a group helping people whose incomes were lost due to the pandemic. Our children and grandchildren all seem to have learned what Jesus said, "It is more blessed to give than receive."

When I began my essay on sex, I talked about hugging and kissing everyone at church I have not been to church for a year. Nor have I hugged or kissed anyone except John, not even family. We have not seen some family members for over a year.

Allegations about sexual abuse seem to have almost disappeared; this doesn't mean it still isn't happening; it's just that the news is now dominated by people dying of the virus. Our church publishes sermons on You-Tube and occasionally we watch preachers on TV. We read something from a Christian author and/or Bible each day. None of this is as rewarding as corporate worship, but it's better than nothing. I miss being involved in groups of people buying gifts for foster children, preparing snacks for first responders, preparing meals for the homeless. At least we can contribute to the few people who are still doing these things. Someday we will return to normal.

Appendix A: How it all began

Texas City, April 16, 1947
Jo Ellen Gill, Milby Senior High School

This essay was awarded second place in the Atlantic Monthly Creative Writing Contest for High School Students. The author was presented a four year scholarship by the University of Pittsburgh.

The popular magazine article said, "Silently and orderly the children filed out of the wrecked buildings. A trail of blood proved that they had calmly and orderly followed their teachers in a straight line, as if participating in a fire drill."

That is not what happened in my fifth-grade classroom at the end of the hall on the second floor. Perhaps there were some who did behave in an orderly manner, but I did not see any of these persons in the mob of hysterical children and teachers that morning of the great explosion.

Earlier that April day I had stood outside the two-story brick elementary school and stared curiously at the orange and purple flame against the clear blue sky. I had asked my teacher what it was, and she said that there was a ship burning down at the docks.

Meanwhile the town's people bustled about as if the fire in the sky were not there at all. It was a warm and sunny spring morning and everyone seemed in a good humor. Wives kissed their husbands good-bye, unaware that they were doing so for the last time, and little boys played hooky from school to visit the docks and watch the ship burn. Only a few realized the danger. While only a few worried executives, perspiring dock hands, and grim-faced firemen were fighting a losing battle, the people in town went about their business, as innocently placid as an animal before the slaughter.

Then it happened. The first sounds I heard were the terrified screams of other children. One moment I had been working long division, and then suddenly I was penned under my desk. The other children were shoving and pushing in a frenzy, all trying to crowd through the narrow doorway at one time. The only person who noticed me and helped me to my feet was Ronald, the biggest and dumbest boy in our class, who had always been the subject of our teasing and joking.

The floors were so slippery with blood and glass that I might have fallen had I not been surrounded by a crowd. The air was hazy and dusty from falling plaster, and I moved down the hall with the mob as if in a dream. Suddenly I heard a groan and saw a teacher holding her face. A piece of flying glass or steel had pierced her eye and it was hanging out of the socket. I saw a man holding a little girl in his arms, trying to shield her from the mob. Another child fainted and was rescued by the janitor from being trampled.

"All right now. Stop that crying. Hush up, I said."; even the loud voice of this teacher could not be easily heard, so she gave up and busied herself wiping the children's bloody wounds with a dirty dust cloth.

The third-graders were trapped in their room and were shrieking and crying, "Let us out, let us o-u-t!" Then they would kick and pound in vain and stick small bloody fists through broken holes in small window panes. Finally a foresighted teacher encouraged them to climb through the transom and jump down on him.

The ceiling buckled and caved in, blocking the nearest stairway. Several children, disregarding shouted orders, slid down the banisters, plowing through the rubble. Finally, we descended another stairway and were herded like a flock of frightened sheep onto the playground. Toward the south I could see the flames leaping higher, blazing as if the whole sky were one mass of fire.

A little bald man was gesturing and shouting, "Go north. Even if you live in the south, go north."

I was fortunate. I lived on the north side of town.

By this time, many townspeople had gathered in the streets, Whole families were walking north, especially the Latin Americans whose homes were in the south. As far as I could see there were olive-skinned people, dressed in bright colored fiesta coats and shawls, carrying their babies and a few prized possessions. They didn't know where they were going. They only knew that their homes had been destroyed. The flames were behind us as we walked. All faces were expressionless, and no one spoke to me. We just walked.

Meanwhile, down at the docks the fire raged on, destroying those who survived the first blast and endangering the lives of the gas-masked rescue workers. Fire trucks were brought in from other cities because all local equipment and those who used it had been destroyed. Twelve men screamed for help from a burning building within which they were trapped. The blazing roof collapsed and nothing more was heard except the hissing and crackling of flames. Rescue workers were instructed to bring in the living and ignore the dead. They couldn't be helped. Pickup trucks lined with blood-soaked mattresses carried the injured to overflowing clinics and hospitals.

The lawns surrounding our two small local clinics were cluttered with wounded and dying, waiting for medical attention. Women of the town joined nurses and Red Cross workers as they tried to relieve the misery as they bent over the stretchers on the sidewalks and lawns. Police blockades were set up to prevent hysterical mobs from entering the area in search of friends and relatives.

In our neighborhood, nearly two miles from the docks, people were more fortunate. Their injuries and damages were less serious. Nevertheless, the neighbors lingered outside their houses, a little afraid to enter the buildings. Since our front door was caved in, blocking the entrance, we, too, mingled with the neighbors to discuss the situation.

Although one woman was suffering from loss of blood, she remained composed. "Tom's dead. I know it."

The women who were binding her poorly sewed wounds tried to be reassuring. "No, he isn't, Myra. Don't say that. You'll find him Myra; or course you will."

She lit a cigarette. "I'll find him in the morgue."

A thin, nervous little man spoke up. "It was sabotage; that's what it was. Someone set off dynamite."

"No, 'twasn't either;. 'twas an atomic bomb. Carlotta's brother-in-law said so, and he ought to know."

"Yeah, there's sure to be a tidal wave. First they blow us up, and now we'll all get washed away."

"I never did like this place. I always said it was dangerous. I always said this would happen. I always knew…"

The plump, frowsy-haired woman raised her voice to a shrill pitch. "I thought it was the boiler in our house. I says to Charlie, I says, you promised to fix that boiler. It's all your fault, and then he says…"

Then there started a whispered rumor among the nervous, white-faced neighbors: "Another blast, another ship, another explosion!" finally the rumor was made a reality by a blaring loudspeaker on an automobile: "Evacuate! Immediately!! Evacuate! Evacuate!"

Reluctantly the people left, still wondering where their loved ones were and dreading to leave without them. We forced my mother into my aunt's car, only after leaving a note and our car for my father if, and when, he should return.

Fourteen miles away we came to the large country home of our friends. When we arrived there was already a large group of women and children. The men had gone to help. I hoped that my father was with them, helping and not lying in a hospital or morgue.

The younger children were squealing and laughing in a game of red rover, but somehow I didn't feel like playing with them. Instead I lingered near the women and listened to their hushed conversation.

The women kept looking at my blood-streaked face and I could hear whispers ,"Poor child. Do you suppose she'll always look like that?" She'll be a social misfit with a face scarred like that."

I had been so horrified at the sight of other people that I hadn't even thought of how I must look. Mother must not have noticed either. Frantically I rushed to a mirror and then felt a little sick at what I saw. Finally I washed my face and discovered with relief that I was only scratched, and that most of the blood which was caked on me was evidently not my own.

In the late afternoon a meal of sandwiches, milk, and strawberry shortcake was prepared. Even though no one had eaten all day, we left this food almost untouched.

In the early evening we saw our car coming up the drive and with a squeal of delight I ran to meet my father. My aunt and my mother had burst into tears when they saw that he was safe. I didn't see why they wanted to cry when they hadn't shed a tear before. He dragged himself out of the car, almost like an old man, and then told of some of the horrors he had seen while working with a rescue crew at the docks.

When night came the children crowded into all available beds. Wedged in between my sister and my friend Nancy, I lay in the dark and listened to the sirens of ambulances on the nearby highway. All night long they wailed and shrieked. I was beginning to doze when I heard a rumble and felt the whole house shake. I knew what it was—the second blast, fourteen miles away!

My friends and I gave up the idea of sleeping and decided to join our parents who were listening to the radio downstairs.

The radio announcer was talking in a fast, terse manner: "The following are dead; the following are missing; the following are injured; the following were treated and released; the following are near death---Anyone knowing the whereabouts of the following, please notify the nearest of kin." Then the announcer would list name after name, many of them familiar to us. On the list of the dead was the name of Myra's husband, our neighbor—Myra who had calmly announced, "Tom's dead. I know it."

Two days later we returned home, swept up glass, and put in temporary windows and doors. Our home was easily repaired but on the homes of those less fortunate I could see red and white cardboard "condemned" signs.

Of all the changes in our town, the ones which impressed me most were the ones in our school. The Salvation Army had taken over the classrooms, the home economics cottage had a free soup line, and the gymnasium was a temporary morgue.

The morgue was a subject of fascination to my brother and me. Each of us dared the other to enter it but neither of us had the nerve; for whenever we came within a block of it, the odor made us ill. Finally, my brother had to deliver a telegram inside the building and he saw some of the sights he had been reading about, mangled bodies with no embalming or refrigeration. After he described the stench to me, I didn't want to even think about the place anymore, much less go there.

The local churches and funeral parlors held services every day. Many of our friends we would never see again. As the days passed, some of the buildings were repaired and replaced, but no one could replace the human lives. School reopened and we tried to live a normal life once more.

"They will forget," people said. "Children get over things quickly."

Remembering now what they said, I think of my first dance in that same gymnasium which had been the morgue. I was excited over the blue net evening dress, my first, and the real corsage from the florist. But once I had started dancing on the smooth polished floor, I could think of nothing but what had lain on that floor, April 1947.

BIOGRAPHY

Jo Ellen Oliver won a college scholarship for her essay, "Texas City, April 16, 1947," sparking her interest in writing. She graduated in English education from the University of Texas and earned two masters' degrees from Auburn University and the University of Georgia in reading education and counseling. She also earned a PhD from the University of Georgia She has had articles in professional journals and has published two books under the pen name of Jillian Wright: The Man Under the Bridge, about homeless people, and Fox Hollow, a mystery-romance. This collection of autobiographical stories is intended to portray changes of attitude over the last century about family, race, and sex.

Oliver is married to Dr. John E. Oliver, a retired professor and veterinary neurologist. They have three children and ten grandchildren.

Warren Sibleyh Cushman, my great grandfather and two of his grandchildren: Gloria Wright, my mother, and her cousin Bob Longfellow.

Warren Cushman, artist, by himself.

Warren Cushman and a friend

John's parents, Col. John and Leatha Oliver and on the left side, Jo Ellen's parents, George M. and Gloria Wright Gill. The bride and groom are JoEllen and John Oliver on December 27, 1957.

Then and Now

Jo Ellen Oliver at middle age

Her sister, Jean Gill, with two of her paintings which won awards.

Jo Ellen Oliver

Jo Ellen

Jo Ellen and John at his Aggie Ring Dance

CPSIA information can be obtained
at www.ICGtesting.com
Printed in the USA
LVHW041352051121
702522LV00001B/41

9 781647 495732